OBAMA AND THE END OF THE AMERICAN DREAM

Obama and The End of the American Dream

Essays in Political and Economic Philosophy

By

Michael A. Peters
The University of Waikato, New Zealand

Postscript by Tina Besley

SENSE PUBLISHERS
ROTTERDAM / BOSTON / TAIPEI

A C.I.P. record for this book is available from the Library of Congress.

ISBN 978-94-6091-769-1 (paperback)
ISBN 978-94-6091-770-7 (hardback)
ISBN 978-94-6091-771-4 (e-book)

Published by: Sense Publishers,
P.O. Box 21858, 3001 AW Rotterdam, The Netherlands
https://www.sensepublishers.com

Printed on acid-free paper

TABLE OF CONTENTS

AMERICAN DREAM IN IMAGES

The American Dream that crystallized around James Truslow Adams' *The epic of America* originally formulated in the early 1930s and conditioned by a decade of complexity and contradiction, of big government projects, intense nationalism, the definition of the American way, and a distinctive collection of American icons – Mickey Mouse, Popeye, the rise of the musical comedy of Broadway, the emergence of the jukebox[1] – also has a visual and image history. Indeed, Adam's dream of opportunity for each according to ability or achievement shaped against the old class culture of Europe emphasizes a vision of social order in which each person can succeed despite their social origins.

The history of the American Dream lends itself to being "narrated" through a sequence of images more so than most histories because America is the home of the moving image ... images is everything; it defines a spectacular culture based on TV, on film – "movies" – and increasingly on the video as it has emerged in the age of YouTube. Image creation, collection, dissemination and management is at the heart of American commerce and culture branding products and companies, ubiquitous advertising that blurs reality and fantasy, and that creates both "the news" and the home theatre.

In considering a selection of images that should embellish this essay I focused on a number of clearly defined sets: the *national symbols* represented in "Old Glory" (the American flag), the Statue of Liberty, the White House and the US Treasury building; the civil rights movements with historic photos of the march on Washington in 1963, photos on Martin Luther King, Robert Kennedy, Lyndon Baines Johnson, "I have a dream" speech, and a sequence of photos documenting the assassination of Martin Luther King at the Lorraine motel in Memphis where he was shot and later was turned into a civil rights museum; a series of photos that focus on housing and home-life and later the sub-prime housing crisis triggering the massive recession in 2007, and the automobile so much a part of America; there are also a deliberate linking of Adam's *The epic of America* and Obama's *The audacity of hope*, as well as photos of Obama remarkable ascendancy to power; finally there are some pictures that indicate the fact that the dream has been shattered.

These image sets are treated largely but not exclusively in consecutive sequence. Had this been a larger book I would have included other sets from Hollywood, the "dream factory," the comic book culture, the architecture, galleries and museums, city-scapes and motorway systems, the massive grand plains and agro-businesses that dominate the uninhabited rural areas, the landmarks and beauty of so much natural landscape.

Michael A. Peters
The University of Waikato, August 28, 2011

NOTES

[1] See "America in the 1930s" at http://xroads.virginia.edu/~1930s/front.html.

ACKNOWLEDGEMENTS

Most of these essays appeared in one form or other in my "column" in the journal *Policy Futures in Education* under the banner "Obama's America" during his first term of office and while I was employed as a professor at the University of Illinois (Urbana-Champaign). These essays were essentially short pieces that made observations on the contemporary political context and use an event to inquire more deeply into the basis of Obama's presidency and the crises he faced. They are also largely now my parting comment on the six years that I was domiciled in the town of Urbana-Champaign while working at the University of Illinois. I was encouraged by my colleagues and students to make these pieces more widely available. I would like to take this opportunity to thank my colleagues and students at Illinois for their encouragement and comments. I would also like to thank Ruth Fearnley at the University of Waikato for reading and proofing the manuscript and Paul Cowan for help with mastering the images. I would also like to acknowledge and thank Tina Besley for the Postscript and Peter de Liefde and Bernice Kelly for the opportunity to publish this work and for the preparation of the book.

Michael A. Peters
University of Waikato
25 April 2012

PROLOGUE

I came to the U.S. at the invitation of the Dean of the Faculty of Education as an excellence hire in 2005 to take up the position of professor in the Department of Educational Policy Studies at the University of Illinois, located in the twin cities of Urbana-Champaign, about an hour and a half south of Chicago. The University of Illinois is a land grant institution, the flagship of the Illinois system and one of the 'big ten' public universities. The University had a great reputation and I accepted the position in part so that I could study at close hand the Chicago School of economics and U.S. neoconservatism. I had been active in the struggle against neoliberalism in New Zealand over the decade of the 1990s and had studied and written about the sources of neoliberalism and its deleterious effects on education and social policy (Peters, 2011).

I had spent the previous five years (2000-2005) at the University of Glasgow helping to establish a new Faculty of Education that had merged the University Educational Studies department with the St Andrews Catholic Teachers' College, a merger that had many difficulties. I was fortunate to hold a personal chair at the University of Auckland, New Zealand and a position as research professor in the new faculty at Glasgow, enabling us to travel between Scotland and New Zealand, spending the winter months of the northern hemisphere in the sunny climes of the Auckland gulf. Glasgow is a great postindustrial city that has reinvented itself from its industrial past that was based on Clyde shipbuilding and other engineering industries, transforming itself into European city of culture in 1990 with its restored Edwardian architecture, its parks, gardens, museums, art galleries (including the Burrell Collection) and retail shopping center second only to London. In 1999 Glasgow was named as the UK's City of Design and Architecture and the Glasgow Science Center was opened in 2001. In 2014 Glasgow is to host the Commonwealth Games. Glasgow is also a working class city that suffered from de-industrialization, urban poverty, depopulation and gentrification of the city that took place within the neoliberal environment of open, competitive and unregulated markets that characterized Thatcher's Britain in the 1980s.

Many of our friends outside the university had grown up in the poor parts of Glasgow like the Gorbals and had strong ties to teaching and to unions. Big Frank Docherty, now a well know and exceptional painter strongly influenced by Magritte and the French surrealists had been the leader of the Scottish teachers' union for many years. The Ubiquitous Chip, our favorite pub, was the gathering place for

1

a group of talented folk that included teachers, lecturers and professors as well as people from other walks of life: a filmmaker, a novelist, a solicitor, a record producer, a gardener, a compositor, an entrepreneur, an engineer, a proofreader, a personnel manager and so on. Many worked for the BBC or the new established Scottish Parliament. All were well read and many also played a musical instrument. They are an amazingly interesting and friendly group of people who grew up in a society that had historically struggled for educational equality and led Europe in its quest for early age literacy among its population. In fact a number of historians have argued that it was strong Scottish literacy, laid down in the parish by virtue of John Knox, that was in part responsible for the Scottish Enlightenment.

Knox was a clergyman, educated at the Universities of St Andrews and Glasgow, who became the leader of the Scottish Reformation in the early sixteenth century and who, together with five other ministers, wrote *The first and second books of discipline* that transformed the Scottish church and nation establishing Presbyterianism in the 1600s against both Catholicism and Anglicanism. Knox, while a hard-line Calvinist, established an appreciation for democracy and literacy and an attitude that welcomed natural law and reason, paving the way for a group of Presbyterian moderate clergy who were able to take over and dominate the Church of Scotland over a century later. This group included Frances Hutcheson and Adam Smith. Hutcheson succeeded Gershom Carmicheal to occupy the Chair of Moral Philosophy at Glasgow in 1729. His moral philosophy, based on the *Essay on the nature and conduct of the passions and affections and illustrations upon the moral sense* published anonymously in 1728, postulated a 'moral sense of beauty in actions and affections, by which we perceive virtue or vice, in ourselves or others' and, among others (including a moral sense of beauty), a public sense – *sensus communis* – 'a determination to be pleased with the happiness of others and to be uneasy at their misery'. He rejected the psychological egoism of Thomas Hobbes and the ethical rationalism of Samuel Clarke and William Wollaston. His ethical theories strongly influenced the thought of Adam Smith and David Hume. Both followed Hutcheson in holding that moral qualities are really sentiments, that is, feelings or emotions. Smith was appointed to the chair of logic and rhetoric at Glasgow in 1751 and a year later took Hutcheson's chair, producing the *Theory of moral sentiments* which appeared in 1759.

I had studied Hume's epistemology as a philosophy student at Auckland in the 1980s. Coming to Glasgow was an ideal opportunity to read his social and political thought and the philosophy of the Scottish Enlightenment. During the weekend of my job interview I read Smith's *Theory of moral sentiments*, his most important philosophical work and ethical basis of his later work, to understand his replacement of Hutcheson's moral 'sense' with psychological motives and his stoical conception of man as both self-interested and self-governed based on principles of natural law.[1] Smith's work demonstrated that our moral ideas and actions are a product of our nature as *social* beings and that while we have a natural tendency to look after ourselves we are also endowed with empathy towards others. Smith left Glasgow in 1764 to take up the position of tutor to a young Scottish noble in France and there he began to write *Inquiry into the nature and causes of the wealth of nations* published 1776.[2] *The wealth of nations* as he writes in Book 1, is concerned with 'the causes of this improvement in the productive powers of nature, and the order, according to which its produce is naturally distributed among the different ranks and conditions of men in the society'. The main argument comes in Book 4 where he argues that the government should leave individuals free to find the most profitable employment of their labor or capital under a system of natural liberty in which individuals pursuing their own legitimate interests unknowingly contribute to the good of the whole.

The first course I taught at Illinois was in the political economy of education focusing on neoliberalism and neoconservativism. The Chicago school under George Stigler and Milton Freidman played up the self-interest angle of Smith's thought at the expense of his much more 'social' understanding of human nature. The Chicago school attempted to restore credibility to the *laissez-faire* policies of the classical school after Keynesianism and Marxism. The course was over-subscribed. I began with the following course description:

Political economy has a disciplinary past that reaches back into the Enlightenment. Unlike traditional economics, which tends to study the economy as a self-contained sphere, political economy deals with the question of legitimate government in relation to the production, distribution and exchange of goods and services. Hence economic concerns can never be entirely divorced from political, social, and cultural ones. This requires a multidisciplinary and not wholly mathematical approach – as is found in traditional economics.

Political economy has a valuable perspective to bring to the understanding of education. It is distinguished by the fact that it starts from a labor theory of value, and brings the study of economics, law and political studies to understanding questions of educational policy, curriculum, and practice. Education has always been understood as part of political economy from its earliest inception, not only as it is related to 'the wealth of nations' and the 'productive powers of labor' but also in relation to how societies conceive of 'rights' and laws. This course will focus on the contemporary political economy of education: we will focus on the topics of education and welfare capitalism; neoliberal reforms in education; and so-called 'Third Way' and neoconservative education policies.

Education has been a part of political economy from its earliest inception, not only related to 'the wealth of nations' and the 'productive powers of labor' but also inscribed in the 'rights of man' and therefore part of the jurisdiction of the modern state. Education as a human right was mentioned in the early prototype for The Declaration of the Rights of Man and the Citizen (1793) and is also assumed in the notion of equality of opportunity which defines a political tradition that weds the French declaration with the U.S. Constitution (1783).

This course, while acknowledging the classical foundations of political economy of education, is oriented to the contemporary scene – the postwar years of the twentieth century and the development of education policy from the Keynesian welfare state settlement period, through the neo-liberalism of the 1980s, to

Figure 1.

Third Way and neo-conservative policies of the first decade of the twenty-first century.

The course began by considering approaches to political economy, including Michel Foucault's governmentality, before focusing on 'social policy, education and the crisis of the welfare state', 'neoliberal counter reforms' with readings on the privatization of education, school choice and accountability, and 'the Third Way and neoconservative education policy. I had focused, in addition, at the end of the course on the writings of Leo Strauss, a Jewish émigré who taught at the University of Chicago from 1949 to his retirement in 1967 and at that time I began research on his work that eventually led to a collection on his work with a Ph.D. student who took the class (York & Peters, 2011). Strauss was perhaps the preeminent conservative political philosopher in America and the source of inspiration for neo-conservatives whose early reputation rested on his work on his lectures on natural law and his attempt to provide a response to historicism and the moral relativism of social sciences.

In this context we must also remember that Barack Obama was a professor (lecturer and senior lecturer) in the Law School at Chicago where he taught constitutional law for 12 years from 1992 until his election to the U.S. Senate in 2004. He was one of the few black professors and he taught due process and equal protection areas of constitutional law, voting rights class that traced the evolution of election law, from the disenfranchisement of blacks to contemporary debates over districting and campaign finance, and his own course on racism and law using sources from Frederick Douglass, W.E.B. Dubois, the Rev. Martin Luther King Jr and Malcolm X as well as classic law cases like Brown v. Board of Education. He was reputedly not close to any one at Chicago, an institution known for its conservative 'hot-house' views, perhaps because he also worked in the State Senate and also at attorney law firm specializing in civil rights litigation and neighborhood economic development. Yet it is clear that he drew many crucial members of his political team from the University of Chicago including Austan Goolsbee who serves as Chairman of his Council of Economic Advisors. It is equally clear that Obama embraced the ethos of the free market and some commentators have indicated that he is sympathetic to Chicago school economics as a result of his days at the University of Chicago.[3]

Obama has had strong connections with the city of Chicago and the State of Illinois for over two decades. He served three terms in the Illinois senate from 1997 to 2004 and he ran successfully for the US Senate becoming a senator from Illinois in 2004. After graduating with a degree in political science from Columbia University in 1981 he took up the job as director of the Developing Communities Project (DCP), working as a community organizer in the South Side of Chicago from 1985 to 1988, before entering Harvard Law School. As a community organizer he set up a job training program, a college preparatory tutoring program, and a tenants' rights organization. He returned to Chicago after graduating with a professional doctorate in law (Juris Doctor) from Harvard in 1991 to accept a two year position at the Chicago Law Faculty to work on his first book *Dreams from my father* (1995). During this period he organized Illinois Project Vote to register unregistered Afro-American voters, and served on boards of directors of the Woods Fund of Chicago, the Joyce Foundation and the Chicago Annenberg Challenge. These charitable foundations centred largely on the Chicago and Great Lakes region focusing on grant making to public school, employment and environmental projects. The Chicago Annenberg Challenge was a Chicago public school reform project from 1995 to 2001. William Ayers, Anne Hallett and Warren Chapman were the three co-authors of Chicago's winning Annenberg Challenge $49.2 million grant proposal in 1995, distributed over five years. Obama was the founding president of the Annenberg Challenge and chairman of the board of directors from 1995 to 1999 having been asked by serve by Patricia Albjerg Graham who served as vice chairman.[4] The Chicago School Reform Collaborative led by Ayers, Hallett and Chapman designed the request for proposals and the Board approved grants for some thirty-five networks representing a total of 170 public schools. The Annenberg Challenge also led to the development of Chicago's first community foundation for public education, the Chicago Public Education Fund, that focused on improving the effectiveness of teachers.

The Annenberg Challenge was strongly criticized by the conservative education Right. The final technical report released in 2003 (Smilie & Wenzel, 2003) indicated that 'the Challenge had little effect on student outcomes' (p. 1) although there was evidence that 'Breakthrough Schools' which received special financial assistance and professional support 'sustained or strengthened aspects of teacher professional community, school leadership and relational trust' (p. 3). Significantly, the Report argued that 'while it may be important to encourage local pluralism and self-determination ..., it is less effective to distribute relatively small amounts of resources among a very large number of schools ...' (p. 5).

Obama retired from the Board of the Annenberg Challenge in 2002 after being reelected to the Illinois Senate. He has had a very strong, consistent and intimate relationship with public education. Strengthening public education has always been a significant part of his politics and his policies.[5] His mother was a teacher and Obama constantly cites his own education case as an improbable story emblematic of the American Dream. Education at all levels has increasingly become responsibilized for moving out of the recession and for long term structural gains aimed at 'winning the future,' a heavy ideological burden for public education to bear.

I remember sitting with a group of friends around the television on election night, all academics and enthusiastic Obama supporters. As a New Zealander I was unable to vote but I accompanied friends to Indiana to do a day's campaigning for Obama in a State known for its revival of the KKK. Election night was a moving and magical occasion and as the votes were counted there was an air of palpable hope as we witnessed history being made with the election of Barack Obama as the first Afro-American president in the United States of America. There was a collective sigh of relief at the end of the Bush era. There was *a return of hope* that was cemented by Obama's acceptance speech and a series of immediate reforms. Hope had been put severely to the test under the neoconservatives who had prosecuted an aggressive foreign policy. Obama had initiated a philosophy of hope based on the ideal of a new ethical community that offered a vision of optimism about progress toward improvement at home and abroad. This principle of hope for Obama was almost the rediscovery of the ontological foundation of a concept of human existence infused by equality and education that defeated the desperation and the despair that accompanied the negative and divisive politics of the previous era to emphasize 'simple dreams' and 'small miracles', the chance to participate in the political process, to heal the differences and to give the next generation of children a better life.

James Kloppenberg (2011) in *Reading Obama: Dreams, hope and the American political tradition* argues that Obama is the product of three distinct developments: the experiment of American democracy that simultaneous made his rise possible and now constrains him; America's contribution to the Western political tradition in the form of pragmatism that defines Obama's sensibilities; and the intellectual upheavals that played out on American campuses during his two decades at Occidental College, Columbia University, Harvard Law School and the University of Chicago Law School that demonstrated the disembodied nature of theory and knowledge from government policy and individual choices, as Obama summed it up in an early essay. Obama, as Kloppenberg (2011) writes, 'showed the capacity and inclination to mobilize America's intellectual traditions to bolster democratic political action' (p. 24).

In March 2011, after the democratic revolutions across the Arab world, the earthquakes in Christchurch, New Zealand and Tōhoku, Japan, the latter that caused a tsunami the likes of which the country had never previously experienced, Obama's version of the American Dream looks distinctively tarnished with little room for movement or reform and not much in the way of international political leadership. The Dream needs international nourishment if is to survive in a digital globalized world yet the Dream is in tatters, and the prospects of Obama winning a second term seems improbable at this point.

The following chapters were written mostly as short pieces for a column called 'Obama's America' for a journal I established while at the University of Glasgow called *Policy futures in education*. These brief essays were designed to provide a clear introduction to issues as they arose and were largely intended for an international audience. A few of the essays appeared as editorials or in other journals. As I leave the University of Illinois to take up a new position at The University of

Waikato in New Zealand, I am struck by the perilous state of the American economy and erosion of funding for the education system. The University of Illinois is owed some $500 million in State receipts by a State government that cannot balance its books and is busy laying off State workers. When I arrived at the university in 2005 over half its income came from the State. Now that figure is less than 18% and the University of Illinois is forced to raise student tuition fees to survive. In a period of six years the university has essentially become a private university dependent on hikes in student fees to cover additional funding. The picture looks bleak indeed for the American system of higher education, as it does for European universities. And yet education is the key to the knowledge economy and to economic survival in the future although its capacity for job creation is in doubt and the old policy mantras require fundamental rethinking.

NOTES

[1] See the full text at http://www.econlib.org/library/Smith/smMS.html.

[2] See the full text at http://www.econlib.org/library/Smith/smWN.html.

[3] See for instance Jodi Kantor's (2008) story ('The long run') in *The New York Times* at http://www.nytimes.com/2008/07/30/us/politics/30law.html?_r=1&ref=politics&pagewanted=all; and Naomi Klein's (2008) 'Beware the Chicago boys' piece in *The Guardian* at http://www.guardian.co.uk/commentisfree/2008/jun/14/barackobama.uselections2008.

[4] Ex-President of the University of Illinois Stan Ikenberry was also a member of the board.

[5] See particularly *The Obama Education Plan* (2009) for a summary of the Obama-Biden education plan and Obama's campaign proposals. In addition see the White House site on education at http://www.whitehouse.gov/issues/education and his voting record at http://www.ontheissues.org/social/barack_obama_education.htm.

REFERENCES

Kloppenberg, J. (2011). In *Reading Obama: Dream, hopes and the American political tradition*. Princeton: Princeton University Press.

Smilie, M. & Wenzel, S. (2003). *The Chicago Annenberg challenge: Successes, failures and lessons for the future*. Consortium on Chicago School Research. At http://ccsr.uchicago.edu/downloads/p62.pdf.

The Obama Education Plan (2009). An *Education Week* Guide. San Francisco: Jossey-Bass.

RENEWING THE AMERICAN DREAM: OBAMA'S POLITICAL PHILOSOPHY

The American moment is not over, but it must be seized anew. We must bring the war to a responsible end and then renew our leadership – military, diplomatic, moral – to confront new threats and capitalize on new opportunities. America cannot meet this century's challenges alone; the world cannot meet them without America. The mission of the United States is to provide global leadership grounded in the understanding that the world shares a common security and a common humanity. (Obama, 2007)

The first African American to do so, Barack Obama was elected President of the United States of America on January 20, 2009, with 52.6% of the popular vote and 364 Electoral College votes to John McCain's 162. His rise to the presidential office has been spectacular: from community organizer and civil rights attorney, to lecturer in constitutional law at the University of Chicago (1992–2004) and leader in the Illinois Senate (1997–2004), to US Senator (2004–2008) and President.

Obama is one of the few presidents born outside the continental mainland and his early background sensitizes him to the world and a global vision that few before have shared or experienced. He was born in Hawaii of a White American mother, Anne Dunham, a field anthropologist, and Barack Hussein Obama, a Black Kenyan father. His parents divorced after three years and Ann Dunham married an Indonesian man, Lolo Soetoro, and the family moved to Jakarta where Obama completed his early schooling before moving back to Hawaii to live with his grandmother. He completed his high school education in Los Angeles before attending Columbia University to study political science and international relations and then after a stint as director of the church-based Developing Communities Project in Chicago he was admitted to Harvard Law School where he was elected as president of the *Law Review*, graduating with a Juris Doctor (J.D.) in 1991.[1]

The bare facts of this remarkable chronology do not do justice to the subtle ways in which Obama's birth and life experiences have shaped his vision for America, for reclaiming the American dream, and his political and economic philosophy. Perhaps, above all, Obama's political philosophy is based on a moral vision informed by his own religious beliefs as a practicing Christian, his experience as a community organizer, his understanding of the law, and a set of democratic ideals enshrined in the best traditions of American political life and exemplified in the speeches of Lincoln, Franklin D. Roosevelt and Kennedy – three presidents to

Figure 2.

whom he refers constantly. The elements of his political philosophy are not hard to discern even if they are not developed as a coherent theory:[2]

- the value of national unity that transcends all divisions – 'one America', the *United* States of America, bipartisanship;
- accordingly, a rejection of 1960s dualisms that have bedeviled American politics since the 1960s – 'Left' & 'Right', 'market' & 'State', 'Black' & 'white' – and a cross-party;
- a narrative of freedom anchored in an awareness of the history of oppression and the corresponding choice of the historical Black Church;
- a theory of community as the basis of democracy, identity and self-transformation;
- a belief in the ethos of community service as an essential component of civic education;
- a philosophy of hope and inclusiveness based on his 'favorite' thinkers – Friedrich Nietzsche, Reinhold Niebuhr and Paul Tillich;
- cosmopolitanism (based on the equal moral worth of all individuals) and a global sensitivity and outlook, with personal experience in Kenya, Indonesia, Hawaii, as well as mainland USA (Chicago, IL, Cambridge Harvard);
- legal constitutionalism and theory of jurisprudence;
- an American pragmatism and experimentalism with a strong emphasis on 'what works';

- open government with an emphasis on ethics and responsibility to change the culture of corruption in Washington;
- a progressivist egalitarian economic philosophy that is a managed form of capitalism oriented to crisis management in the short term – with massive government assistance to banks, the middle class, and businesses as well as huge infrastructure investment aimed at economic recovery – and market-friendly innovation policies based on the reform of science, technology and energy policies and structural reforms (green energy and universal health care) in the long term.

To sum, Obama's political philosophy is based on the notions of unity, community, equality and hope. He wants to transcend all divisions, to provide a new universalism of provision and encourage a greater inclusiveness that moves beyond the dualism and dichotomies that haunt the USA going back to the 1960s – White–Black, male–female, Democrat–Republican – in order to assert a new unity, the *United* States of America, as he emphasizes. This is a theme going back well before his rise to President when Obama (2004) said:

alongside our famous individualism, there's another ingredient in the American saga. A belief that we are connected as one people. If there's a child on the south side of Chicago who can't read, that matters to me, even if it's not my child. If there's a senior citizen somewhere who can't pay for her prescription and has to choose between medicine and the rent, that makes my life poorer, even if it's not my grandmother. If there's an Arab American family being rounded up without benefit of an attorney or due process, that threatens my civil liberties. It's that fundamental belief – I am my brother's keeper, I am my sister's keeper – that makes this country work. It's what allows us to pursue our individual dreams, yet still come together as a single American family. 'E pluribus unum'. Out of many, one.

It is not clear that we can talk of a theory of community but Obama embraces a form of communitarianism that holds that individual rights must be circumscribed by the communal, with all the cross-generational, religious and patriotic obligations that implies. It also implies that government and corporations are bound by obligations to citizens, like a clean environment, education and health care. As is now well known, Obama was exposed to an activist communitarianism while working as a community organizer in Chicago. Saul Alinsky was the radical non-socialist organizer who inspired community organizations under which Obama worked. Alinsky's (1971) *Rules for Radicals: a pragmatic primer for realistic radicals* was the community organizers' bible and Chicago the birthplace of grass-roots community activism in America, especially through the 1970s and 1980s.[3] (Among his tactics Alinski recommended: 'Power is not only what you have but what the enemy thinks you have'; 'Never go outside the experience of your people'.[4])

The religious dimension of Obama's thought helped to anchor and provide a 'vessel' for his beliefs. In 'Call to Renewal' (Keynote Address, Wednesday, June 28, 2006[5]) he writes about his spiritual dilemma, the 'historical Black Church' and the 'the power of the African-American religious tradition to spur social change':

Figure 3.

It wasn't until after college, when I went to Chicago to work as a community organizer for a group of Christian churches, that I confronted my own spiritual dilemma. I was working with churches, and the Christians who I worked with recognized themselves in me. They saw that I knew their Book and that I shared their values and sang their songs. But they sensed that a part of me remained removed, detached, that I was an observer in their midst. And in time, I came to realize that something was missing as well – that without a vessel for my beliefs, without a commitment to a particular community of faith, at some level I would always remain apart, and alone.

At that time Obama tells us he came to understand the special historical mission of the Black Church, the biblical commitment to equality, and 'its historical struggles for freedom and the rights of man', as a source of hope and political agency. This understanding underscored the importance for Obama that 'values and culture play in some of our most urgent social problems'. He argues that 'the problems of poverty and racism, the uninsured and the unemployed, are not simply technical problems' but 'rooted in our moral imperfections'. In making this claim Obama mentions the great reformers, 'Frederick Douglas, Abraham Lincoln, Williams Jennings Bryant, Dorothy Day, Martin Luther King', 'were not only motivated by faith, but repeatedly used religious language to argue for their cause'. Personal morality is an inescapable part of the constitution of the public, as 'law is by definition a codification of morality, much of it grounded in the Judeo-Christian tradition'.

Figure 4.

Democracy is the process by which religion-specific values translate into universal values and become amenable to reason and justification.

The call to faith and the 'grounding of faith in struggle' enables us to address issues in moral terms and to deny the radical religious right their sway. We cannot 'leave our beliefs at the door before entering the public square' as the secularists would have us believe and US history and separation of Church and State, at least on Obama's reading, indicate the Christian origins of the Constitution. The political question is how we build on 'still-tentative partnerships between religious and secular people of good will'. As he acknowledges, the USA is no longer solely a Christian nation and, accordingly, we have to recognize a new democratic pluralism that reconciles faith and reason, at the cost of rescinding the Bible's inerrancy as a determining article of faith, in the hope of overcoming religious prejudices.

Six weeks into the presidency, the Obama administration had moved swiftly on multiple fronts: the appointment of a full team of executive and policy positions; the winning of a massive stimulus package; the second installment of TARP (Troubled Assets Relief Program); the preparation of the first budget, addressing the deficit and external debt; the bailout of various banks, States and industries; the shoring up of the financial system; the administration of tax cuts; the closure of Guantanamo Bay and ending torture policy; ending the Iraq war and redirecting forces and strategy in Afghanistan; and the innumerable summits (e.g. with governors and mayors). It was a busy time and Obama seemingly travelled everywhere explaining his policies to the American people. He geared up to introduce his economic, health care, energy, and education policies in the delivery of his first budget.[6] In 'The President's Message' he first outlined the dimensions of the economic crisis and then suggested, 'The time has come to usher in a new era – a new era of responsibility in which we act not only to save and create new jobs, but also to lay a new foundation of growth upon which we can renew the promise of America'. He talked of 'our market economy' but noted the necessity of a short-term government 'boost' before outlining 'the long overdue investments in priorities – like clean energy, education, health care, and a new infrastructure'. Education figured strongly in his message and he indicated:

> To give our children a fair shot to thrive in a global, information-age economy, we will equip thousands of schools, community colleges, and universities with 21st Century classrooms, labs, and libraries. We'll provide new technology and new training for teachers so that students in Chicago and Boston can compete with kids in Beijing for the high-tech, high-wage jobs of the future. We will invest in innovation, and open the doors of college to millions of students. We will pursue new reforms – lifting standards in our schools and recruiting, training, and rewarding a new generation of teachers. And in an era of skyrocketing college tuitions, we will make sure that the doors of college remain open to children from all walks of life.

In six weeks, remarkably, he moved on all campaign promises and at least begun the process of change across the board. Yet even now, as then, it is still much too early to tell how successful his policies will be or whether Obama will be able to renew the American dream.

NOTES

[1] Much has already been written on Obama in the pre-presidential stage; see Zutter (1995), Curry (2004), Koltun (2005), Graff (2006), Wallace-Wells (2007), Lizza (2007), MacFarquhar (2007), Mundy (2007).

[2] See, for example, Robert Kuttner (2009).

[3] See 'The Democratic Promise: Saul Alinski and his legacy' at http://www.itvs.org/democraticpromise/alinsky.html.

[4] See http://www.semcosh.org/AlinskyTactics.htm.

[5] http://obama.senate.gov/speech/060628-call_to_renewal/.

[6] For the first budget, entitled 'A New Era of Responsibility: The 2010 Budget', see http://www.whitehouse.gov/omb/.

REFERENCES

Alinsky, Saul D. (1971). *Rules for radicals: A pragmatic primer for realistic radicals*. New York: Random House.

Curry, Jessica (2004). Barack Obama: Under the lights, *Chicago Life*, Fall.

Graff, Garrett (2006). The legend of Barack Obama, *Washingtonian*, November 1.

Koltun, Dave (2005). The 2004 Illinois Senate race: Obama wins open seat and becomes national political 'star', in Sunhil Ahua & Robert Dewhirst (Eds), *The road to Congress 2004*. Haupauge, New York: Nova Science Publishers.

Kuttner, Robert (2009). Obama's economic opportunity: The dismal state of the economy presents Obama with the chance not just to produce a recovery but to restore a more egalitarian society – and a progressive majority, *The American Prospect*. http://www.prospect.org/cs/articles?article=obamas_economic_opportunity.

Lizza, Ryan (2007). Above the fray, *GQ*, September. http://men.style.com/gq/features/landing?id=content_5841.

MacFarquhar, Larissa (2007). The conciliator: Where is Barack Obama coming from? *New Yorker*, May 7. http://www.newyorker.com/reporting/2007/05/07/070507fa_fact_macfarquhar

Mundy, Liza (2007). A series of fortunate events, *The Washington Post Magazine*, August 12.

Obama, Barack (2004). Democratic National Convention in 2004. http://www.librarian.net/dnc/speeches/obama.txt.

Obama, Barack (2007). Renewing American leadership, *Foreign Affairs*, July/August. http://www.foreignaffairs.org/20070701faessay86401/barack-obama/renewing-americanleadership.html.

Wallace-Wells, Ben (2007). Destiny's child, *Rolling Stone*, February 7. http://www.rollingstone.com/politics/story/13390609/campaign_08_the_radical_roots_of_barack_obama.

Zutter, Hank De (1995). What makes Obama run, *Chicago Reader*, December 8. http://www.chicagoreader.com/features/stories/archive/barackobama/.

CHAPTER 2

AUTOMOBILISM, AMERICANISM AND THE END OF FORDISM

2009 was a critical year for the American automobile industry as the world economic slump forced a major restructuring of the 'Big Three' – General Motors, Ford and Chrysler – and placed the long-term future survival of the industry in jeopardy. The Big Three had a combined U.S. market share of 51.8% in December 2007 but as of October 2008, their market share declined by 5.3% to 46.5%. During that same nine-month period, Toyota and Honda increased their U.S. market shares by 3.1% to a combined 28.4%. In 2007, the Big Three sold 18 million autos for $387.5 billion whereas Toyota and Honda sold 12.2 millions autos for $304 billion.[1] The globalization of the international automobile marketplace and the emergence of Japanese and South Korean auto-transplants in North America together with the adoption of new flexible production methods suggest that the prospects for renewal of North American auto manufacturing in the face of global competition has come to an unavoidable impasse. These global competition problems are heightened by the role of union labor in the reorganization of the workplace and the technological advances developed by competitors invested in the new hybrids.

These are not trivial problems. At a time of economic crisis and rapidly rising unemployment it had not escaped the attention of commentators that in the U.S. alone the Big Three directly employed 242,000 people and an estimated 2.5 to 3 million indirectly. In the worst slump in the automarket for 36 years the Big Three tried to recover from their botched attempt in December 2008 to seek an expanded $34 billion bailout and were required to submit extensive restructuring plans and concession commitments from unions and bondholders to an inter-agency task headed up by Timothy Geithner and Lawrence Summers.

The automobile industry is not just an employer of 3 million people; the automobile plays a significant role in American myth and reality, shaping an experience that was 20th century industrialism, defining the American dream and embedding the ideology 'automobilism' that puts a premium on the mobility of the individualized self in modern society where the ideal is one car per person of driving age. Now three-car garages are no longer sufficient, or at least they were not before the subprime housing crisis – everyone must have a vehicle, Mom, Dad, and each of the children as they come of driving age. Dad might have in addition a truck or pickup and there might be other means of auto-mobility such as motorbikes, as well. Driving around California one sees automobiles parked behind each other in the

Figure 5.

driveway and before the slump the demand for 5-car garages was rapidly becoming the norm for the middle class.

Henry Ford founded the Ford Motor Company in 1903 experimenting with and institutionalizing the assembly line as an essential part of mass production. The model T was introduced in 1908 and sold for $825 becoming progressively cheaper every year. By 1914 sales were in excess of 250,000. With flagging sales, Ford introduced the Model A in 1927 and sold over four million by 1931. In *My life and work*, Henry Ford (1922) set forth the principles of his *service* that defined his brand of welfare capitalism: (1) An absence of fear of the future or of veneration for the past; (2) A disregard of competition; (3) The putting of service before profit; (4) Manufacturing is not buying low and selling high.[2]

Ford argued 'We must have production, but it is the spirit behind it that counts most. That kind of production which is a service inevitably follows a real desire to be of service'. He also suggested that:

> To make the yield of the earth, in all its forms, large enough and dependable enough to serve as the basis for real life – the life which is more than eating and sleeping – is the highest service. That is the real foundation for an economic system.

He went on to argue that the problem of production has been solved and the material mode of our life is provided for and he warned:

> But we are too wrapped up in the things we are doing – we are not enough concerned with the reasons why we do them. Our whole competitive system, our whole creative expression, all the play of our faculties seem to be centred around material production and its by-products of success and wealth.

Ford was a notorious anti-Semite (Ford, 1920; Baldwin, 2002) and anti-democrat yet his life and work was emblematic of Americanism; of the search for sources of modern identity in consumerism, the optimism of technology to solve all problems, the tension between freedom and authority, the emphasis on invention and practicality, and the respect for rural traditions and the obsessive quest for efficiency (Watts, 2005). Ford's ideal of self-fulfillment through mobility was the basis for a consumer system based on advertising that matched a tide of ever-increasing consumer demand with the principles of mass production. In essence, it defined American capitalism, the individualism of America society (one person, one car), the dream of leisure and freedom from drudgery at work. It also contributed to the 'Five-Dollar Day' that reformed labor in manufacturing by doubling the existing wage.

In 1934 in an insightful essay in the *Prison notebooks*, Antonio Gramsci (1971) defined Americanism as 'mechanicist', crude, brutal – 'pure action' in other words – and contrasted it with tradition. He attempted to demonstrate how Fordism was destructive of trade unions leading to a crisis in high wages, hegemony at the point of production, and the production of new Taylorized workers. Fordist production, entailing an intensified industrial division of labor and assembly line flow of work with increasingly specified tasks by management, increased the potential for capitalist control over the pace and intensity of work and led to the displacement of craft-based production in which skilled laborers exercised substantial control over their conditions of work.

'Fordism' came to define an economic and social system based on the shift from craft to mass production that led to higher levels of material advancement especially throughout the 1940s–60s, only to give way to forms of post-Fordism as new forms of flexible specialization, just-in-time manufacturing and 'total quality management' based on the Japanese experience came to predominate. Post-Fordism arose as a response to globalization of consumer markets and as a new form of flexibility that made greater use of the prospects for customization and personalization made available though new information technologies. Whether this shift represents a new 'techno-economic paradigm', a new 'regime of accumulation' or a new form of production and consumption, clearly there have been changes in demand and in the perception of consumers who are no longer regarded as an undifferentiated mass market but rather highly segmented accordingly to income, preference, age and gender, among other variables (Ash, 1994; Koch, 2006). In one sense the change comes from increasingly complex patterns of consumption driving changes to the production system and greater customer involvement in the production process (rather than vice versa).

Yet Ford also had serious misgivings about the effects of mass automobilism and the materialism it spread. Fordism defined more than the dream of automobilism as a society system permitting freedom of movement and a commensurate 'lifestyle'. The mass production of the automobile to a large extent determined the massive infrastructure investment and building that accompanied superhighway construction and the design and growth of cities and suburbs across America; it defined urban, household and personal space and tutored spatial sensibilities. The 'drive-in' came to epitomize convenience in entertainment, banking, and shopping. In 1910 the U.S. had 8,000 cars and 144 miles of paved roads; by 1985 there were

Figure 6.

over 395 million passenger cars and 109 million commercial vehicles worldwide. There were approximately 600 million miles of roads in the world in 1997, a figure expected to double in 30 years.[3]

These frightening figures have led a host of commentators to criticize the U.S. as the 'Asphalt Nation' (e.g., Kay, 1998) and to emphasize how the automobile has ravaged America's cities and landscape over the past 100 years. Others have taken a radical stand to argue that 'car culture' is unsustainable and that we must move to new cultural practices (Graves-Brown, 1997). Tim Dant and Peter Martin (1999), echo Hawkins (1986) in bemoaning the lack of sociological interest in the car and its impact and the predictable condemnation of the car form of personal transport that many sociologists claim accelerate the decline of community and further atrophy social solidarity and increase trends towards individualization. John Urry (2004) has theorized the impact of 'automobility' that reconfigures civil society, involving distinct ways of dwelling, travelling and socialising in, and through, an automobilized time-space. Urry identifies six components of automobility, or the 'social and technical system of the car': manufactured object; individual consumption; machinic complex; quasiprivate mobility; culture; and environmental resource-use (Urry 2004). While car culture reinforces globalization there is little chance that there will be any large-scale replacement of the demand for real, corporeal, individual travel in the foreseeable future. Urry is concerned with how to conceptualize and theorize the nature of the 'car system' by reference to the notion of systems as self-reproducing or autopoietic in particular, in order to understand the origins of the 20th-century car system and its astonishing expansion across the globe.

In 2009, the White House strongly indicated that the U.S. auto industry must undergo a broad restructuring, requiring sacrifice on the part of autoworkers, creditors, shareholders and the executives who run the companies, if it was to thrive again. GM and Chrysler were required to submit their so-called viability plans as a condition for receiving $17.4 billion in federal loans and being eligible for billions

Figure 7.

more in the future but Ford has not sought government loans. It is clear that the White House could not allow the Big Three to fail, although auto executives were reluctant to contemplate Chapter 11 because they claimed that consumers would not buy from a bankrupt company. It was equally clear that U.S. automanufacturing system was poised at a critical historical juncture, a symbolic watershed – 'the end of Fordism'. In face of the economic downturn and intensified global competition, perhaps this moment provides the opportunity and beginning of a new flexible, responsive, customized manufacturing regime that builds fuel efficient hybrid IT-smart vehicles based on a state-aided total restructuring of the industry, with new investment and market development, new models and product lines, and the diversification beyond motor vehicles.

The Obama administration made substantial pre-election commitments to what Emma Rothschild (2009) calls the 'post-auto-industrial society' based on his energy policy and the prospect of a low-carbon economy. The new energy plan looks to invest $150 billion over ten years for a clean energy future with a commitment to 5 million 'green jobs' and to putting one million plug-in hybrids on the road by 2015 as well as reducing gas emissions. One estimate for jobs in the expanding green economy is promising (Pollin & Wicks-Lim, 2008) and there is no doubt that the new information technologies can greatly assist not only design terms but also in collapsing spaces between work and home, home and all kinds of services from travel to entertainment and shopping.

Yet Rothschild (2009) argues convincingly that the bail out and restructuring needs to be organized around the revitalization of urban and public infrastructure including public transportation that specifically caters to those who have long suffered immobility, long waiting times and poor connections between different modes of transport. This points to the entrenched difficulty of 'automobilism' as an ideology and as a policy problem – it is so connected to many other policy areas that a change is needed in culture and worldview in order to harness all resources to tackle the network of related problems in energy, public transport, urban design, economy, technology and education.

President Obama announced his auto plan (30th March, 2009) saying that he was 'absolutely committed' to the survival of the industry both at home and internationally but remarking 'our auto industry is not moving in the right direction fast enough'. On those grounds he denied further long-term federal bailouts for General Motors (GM) and Chrysler, indicating that all stakeholders needed to make further concessions and clearer restructuring plans were required. GM and Chrysler received $13.4 billion and $4 billion in government loans in February 2009 and were looking for a further $16.6 billion and $5 billion respectively. He also did not dismiss the possibility of controlled bankruptcy while indicating the government would act as guarantor. In an extraordinary move the Obama administration also forced the retirement of Rick Waggoner as CEO of General Motors who was resistant to change and whose focus on the big gas-guzzlers production lines of trucks, Hummers and CRVs flew in the face of Obama's green energy emphasis on smaller, energy-efficient and more customer-responsive vehicles. GM had 60 days to come up with a more acceptable reorganization plan and Chrysler had 30 days to sort out obstacles to the merger with the innovative and highly successful Italian Automaker Fiat if it was to receive $6 billion in government bail-out funds. So far, the auto industry – reputedly employing 3 million – lost 400,000 jobs in one year and both companies (employing some 140,000 in the U.S.) were expected to announce further layoffs. On reflection, the auto industry miraculously was turned around. After filing for a Chapter 11 bankruptcy in 2009, Chrysler and GM have come out of bankruptcy and government-mandated restructuring. The big three had to contend with a recession and trying to be viable with projected U.S. auto sales of about $11 million compared to a heyday of $16 million or more. This is a remarkable turnaround given that the auto industry is a highly centralized market with roughly 10 global automakers accounting for over 77% of total production worldwide. In 2010, GM had a 19.1% market share in the U.S., followed by Ford with a 16.7% market share, Toyato with a 15.2% market share, Honda with a 10.6% market share, Chrysler-Fiat with a 9.4% market share and Nissan with a 7.8% market share. The Detroit comeback was remarkable given that they had lost consumer confidence in 2009 after they were severely hit by the global economic crisis. The crisis also exposed their product portfolio, which was unresponsive to market demand, lacked up-to-date engineering and the flexibility required in a volatile oil market. Obama's handling of this crisis deserves greater recognition even if Asian countries, especially China and India, are predicted to account for 40% of growth in the auto industry over the next five to seven years. Automobilism, no longer solely American, has truly gone global and the U.S. has demonstrated its regenerative capacity with a new generation of information-based service industries.

NOTES

[1] These figures are based on a December 3rd 2008 press release at http://www.procon.org. This source also revealed that Ford received a $1.29 billion tax refund in 2007 while General Motors paid $37.16 billion in 2007 taxes.

[2] This is an abbreviated statement that is referred to in the first and last chapter, taken from the The Project Gutenberg EBook at http://www.gutenberg.org/etext/7213.

[3] See 'The Number of Cars' at http://hypertextbook.com/facts/2001/MarinaStasenko.shtml.

REFERENCES

Amin, Ash (1994). *Post-fordism: A reader*. Blackwell Publishing.

Baldwin, N. (2002). *Henry Ford and the Jews: The mass production of hate*. Public Affairs.

Dant, T. & Martin, P. (1999). By car: Carrying modern society, available at http://www.lancs.ac.uk/staff/dant/by%20car.pdf.

Ford, H. (1920). *The international Jews: The world's foremost problem*, Michigan: Dearborn Publishing.

Ford, H. (1922). *My life and work*, The Project Gutenberg EBook at http://www.gutenberg.org/etext/7213.

Gramsci, Antonio (1971). Americanism and Fordism. In *Selections from the Prison Notebooks* (pp. 277-318), trans. Q. Hoare and G. Nowell Smith, New York: International Publishers.

Graves-Brown, P. (1997). From highway to superhighway: The sustainability, symbolism and situated practices of car culture, *Social Analysis, 41*, 64-75.

Kay, Jane Holtz (1998). *Asphalt nation: How the automobile took over America, and how we can take it back*, University of California Press.

Pollin, R. & Wicks-Lim, J. (2008), Job opportunities for the green economy: A state-by-state picture of occupations that gain from green investments, Amherst: Political Economy Research Institute University of Massachusetts, at http://www.americanprogress.org/issues/2008/06/pdf/green_jobs.pdf.

Rothschild, Emma (2009, February 26). Can we transform the auto-industrial society, *New York Review of Books, LVI*(3), 8-9.

Urry, John (2004). The 'system' of automobility, *Theory, Culture & Society, 21*(4-5), 25-39.

Watts, Steven (2005). *The people's tycoon: Henry Ford and the American century*, New York: Knoff.

OBAMA'S HEALTH REFORMS AND THE LIMITS OF PUBLIC REASON

Edward Kennedy, the great liberal senator from Massachusetts, has died at 77 and with him an era of American politics that was marked by bipartisanship and by a less strident tone, when the GOP had not yet succumbed to the fundamentalist right. He was, as most commentators know, a man who was committed to universal health reform and determined to provide health insurance for all Americans as part of the American dream and 'the cause of his life'. Immediately following, it was not clear whether Kennedy's death would propel, delay or derail the proposed health reforms. Some argued that Obama has over-estimated the public's reception of Truman- or Roosevelt-style government intervention. The actual substance of the reforms is not my real concern here. For the record the official government website[1] mentions that the Administration believes that comprehensive health reform should:

- Reduce long-term growth of health care costs for businesses and government.
- Protect families from bankruptcy or debt because of health care costs.
- Guarantee choice of doctors and health plans.
- Invest in prevention and wellness.
- Improve patient safety and quality of care.
- Assure affordable, quality health coverage for all Americans.
- Maintain coverage when you change or lose your job.
- End barriers to coverage for people with pre-existing medical conditions.

The economics of health care reform is not easy to understand but Obama has indicated on many occasions that it is a ticking time bomb for the American economy. He has also sped up his efforts significantly in June 2009 in order to secure major reform by the end of October of the same year and in the process to prevent the unraveling of the process as public anxiety grows and the agitators have more time to spread the panic. Everyone remembers that in 1993 the Republicans managed to derail Clinton's effort at comprehensive reform, although this may have been due also to other factors.[2]

The details of the reforms are not my focus so much as the process and also the tenor of American politics over this issue. The health reforms are proving to be a stumbling block for the President and in August 2009 he was about ready to jettison his efforts at bipartisanship as right-wing Republicans sowed fear of big government and encouraged the increasingly angry and bitter tone that at that

Figure 8.

time was characterizing the agitated grass-roots opposition. Rush Limbaugh and other conservative media and bloggers have been ranting, calling the president everything from a socialist to a Marxist to a racist. The problem is that the Republican media commentators and bloggers are whipping the extreme fringe into a frenzy of revenge, hatred and violence. David Frum, the conservative commentator acknowledges:

> The Nazi comparisons from Rush Limbaugh; broadcaster Mark Levin asserting that President Obama is "literally at war with the American people"; former vice presidential candidate Sarah Palin claiming that the president was planning "death panels" to extirpate the aged and disabled; the charges that the president is a fascist, a socialist, a Marxist, an illegitimate Kenyan fraud, that he "harbors a deep resentment of America", that he feels a "deep-seated hatred of white people", that his government is preparing "concentration camps, that it is operating snitch lines, that it is planning to wipe away American liberties". All this hysterical and provocative talk invites, incites and prepares a prefabricated justification for violence.[3]

The visual media provide some incontrovertible evidence.

The fact is that this hysteria, hate and threat of violence have become a characteristic of contemporary American politics which is now as fiercely polarized as it has ever been. Where are the rational principles of public debate? What is the role of evidence in these discussions? To what extent is any can we rely on fair representation?

In asking these questions I am reminded of Thomas Kuhn's (1962) *The structure of scientific revolutions* where he came to question the then classic picture of scientific rationality as one that proceeded on the basis of logic and the progressive accumulation of facts. He explains through historical examples that so-called 'normal science' constitutes a paradigm where scientists carry out normal puzzle-solving activities. When the paradigm is stretched to its limits and anomalies begin to pile up, the hard core of the program – based on a set of metaphysical beliefs – is protected from criticism and revision. The anomalies are dismissed on all sorts of grounds until the crisis can no longer be tolerated and scientists break ranks to join the bold ones who have already embarked upon a new revolutionary paradigm that solved the problems of its predecessor. What is more, Kuhn provides a picture of paradigm shift based essentially on nonrational factors. He describes the process as similar to one of religious conversion and calls it a 'gestalt switch'. Kuhn's arguments are too complex to review or evaluate here but his book changed the course of philosophy of science, views of scientific 'progress', and was the single most quoted book in citations in the Arts and Humanities up until quite recently.

If practicing scientists have difficulty relinquishing their favorite theories and beliefs on the basis of evidence, then what hope is there for the ordinary citizen? My experience in academia is that often the evidential process runs the wrong way around: academics often work backwards from their cherished beliefs to find evidence for them rather than to test them out. People are invested in their beliefs and will continue to hold them even in view of incontrovertible evidence. This understanding is part of the new psychology of belief. It is fundamental to understanding the opposition to new ideas and new theories; it is part of the historical understanding of the treatment of the work of Galileo, Darwin, Einstein and many others. Most of the cases in one way or other involve religion and so-called fundamentalist views, not restricted to forms of Christianity. There is a new contest between atheists and fundamentalists that has been marked by the publication of Richard Dawkins' unsubtle *The god delusion*. The new psychology begins by investigating false beliefs and why people hold them. For instance, the group of researchers examines the strength of the belief among many Americans that Saddam Hussein was linked to the terrorist attacks of September 11, identifying a number of social psychological mechanisms voters use to maintain false beliefs in the face of disconfirming information.[4] Their *social psychological* explanation, drawing 'a psychological model of information processing that scholars have labeled motivated reasoning', suggests that the main cause for 'misperception is not the presence or absence of correct information but a respondent's willingness to believe particular kinds of information'. They go on to explain:

> This model envisions respondents as processing and responding to information defensively, accepting and seeking out confirming information, while ignoring, discrediting the source of, or arguing against the substance of contrary information ... Recent literature on motivated reasoning builds on cognitive dissonance

Figure 9.

theory to explain *how* citizens relieve cognitive dissonance: they avoid inconsistency, ignore challenging information altogether, discredit the information source, or argue substantively against the challenge.[5]

An understanding of the psychology of belief is essential not only to education and educators, it is necessary to understand the limits of public reason and public learning processes in general.

NOTES

[1] See http://www.healthreform.gov/.

[2] Theodore Mamor and Jonathon Oberlander's review of Tom Daschle's *Critical: What we can do about the health-care crisis* for the *New York Review of Books* is an accessible and insightful account, http://www.nybooks.com/articles/22931. They believe that Obama's team has a 'good chance' of winning passage for the legislation, although this was before the death of Ted Kennedy.

[3] See http://www.theweek.com/bullpen/column/99474/The_reckless_Right_courts_violence.

[4] See Monica Prasad, Andrew J. Perrin, Kieran Bezila, Steve G. Hoffman, Kate Kindleberger, Kim Manturuk, & Ashleigh Smith Powers (2009). There must be a reason: Osama, Saddam, and inferred justification, *Sociological Review*, 79(2), 142-162. Abstract at http://www3.interscience.wiley.com/journal/122260824/abstract; see the pdf at http://sociology.buffalo.edu/documents/hoffmansocinquiry article_000.pdf.

[5] Some of their references are: DiMaggio, Paul (1997). Culture and cognition, *Annual Review of Sociology*, 23, 263-87; Lodge, Milton & Charles Tabor (2000). Three steps toward a theory of motivated political reasoning. In A. Lupia, M.D. McCubbins, & S.L. Popkin (Eds), *Elements of reason: Cognition, choice, and the bounds of rationality* (pp. 183-213). Cambridge, UK: Cambridge University Press; Perrin, Andrew J. (2006). *Citizen speak: The democratic imagination in American life*. Chicago, IL: The University of Chicago Press; Sunstein, Cass R. (2000). Deliberative trouble?: Why groups go to extremes. *The Yale Law Journal, 110*, 71-119.

ECONOMICS TRUMPS POLITICS; MARKET TRUMPS DEMOCRACY

The U.S. Supreme Court's Decision on Campaign Financing

In the appeal of *Citizens United v. Federal Election Commission* 2009, the U.S. Supreme Court decided on January 29 in a vote 5-4 to overturn existing the Bipartisan Campaign Reform (McCain-Feingold) Act of 2002(BCRA). BCRA is a federal law that prohibits corporations and unions from using their general treasury funds to make independent expenditures for speech that is an 'electioneering communication' or for speech that expressly advocates the election or defeat of a candidate. Citizens United (CU), a nonprofit corporation, released a documentary critical of then-Senator Hillary Clinton, a candidate for her party's Presidential nomination. Assuming that the documentary would run on cable television 30 days before the election, CU produced advertisements. §441b defines an electioneering communication as 'any broadcast, cable, or satellite communication' that 'refers to a clearly identified candidate for Federal office' and is made within 30 days of a primary election. CU, the appellant in the dispute, argued that the documentary was unconstitutional in terms of §441b and to the reporting and disclosure requirements of BCRA. CU sought an injunction on the ground that the documentary was not an 'electioneering communication' because it was not publicly distributed. Perhaps, more importantly, CU held that the case could not be resolved on narrower grounds without restriction political speech – which runs counter to the First Amendment.[1] The Court had to consider the continuing effect of the speech suppression upheld in *Austin v. Michigan Chamber of Commerce*. This was the case in which the Supreme Court held the Michigan Campaign Finance Act which prohibited corporations from using treasury money to support or oppose candidates in elections did not violate the First and Fourteenth Amendments. The Court upheld the restriction on corporate speech based on the notion that '[c]orporate wealth can unfairly influence elections', and the Michigan law still allowed the corporation to make contributions from a segregated fund. The result of the Court's decision was to overrule *Austin*. Chief Justice Roberts, with whom Justice Alito agreed, wrote:

> The Government urges us in this case to uphold a direct prohibition on political speech. It asks us to embrace a theory of the First Amendment that would allow censorship not only of television and radio broadcasts, but of pamphlets, posters, the Internet, and virtually any other medium that corporations and unions might find useful in expressing their views on matters of public concern. Its

theory, if accepted, would empower the Government to prohibit newspapers from running editorials or opinion pieces supporting or opposing candidates for office, so long as the newspapers were owned by corporations – as the major ones are. First Amendment rights could be confined to individuals, subverting the vibrant public discourse that is at the foundation of our democracy (http://supremecourtus.gov/opinions/09pdf/08-205.pdf).

The First Amendment to the U.S. Constitution, which is part of the Bill of Rights, prohibits Congress from making laws that infringe on the freedom to speech. Its major tests of constitutionality has included sedition, war protests, commercial speech, obscenity and pornography, hate speech, and political speech, especially campaign finance reform. The Court originally upheld the law of the Federal Election Campaign Act 1971 that restricted the monetary contributions that may be made to political campaigns and expenditure by candidates. In *Buckley v. Valeo* 424 US. 1 (1976) the Court concluded that limits on campaign contributions 'serve[d] the basic governmental interest in safeguarding the integrity of the electoral process without directly impinging upon the rights of individual citizens and candidates to engage in political debate and discussion'. In *McConnell v. Federal Election Commission*, 540 U.S. 93 (2003) the Court upheld provisions barring the raising of 'soft money' by national parties and the use of soft money by private organizations to finance certain advertisements related to elections. The Court's current ruling has overturned Federal restrictions on corporate electoral advocacy under the BCRA claiming that these are unconstitutional for violating the Free Speech Clause of the First Amendment. *Austin* had previously held that a law that prohibited corporations from using treasury money to support or oppose candidates in elections did not violate the First or Fourteen Amendments. Clearly, the Court's decision has overruled a longtime precedent opposing the use of funds for political advocacy by associations of people. Corporate executives do not require shareholders approval for a political expenditure nor do they need to make any political disclosure. What will the effect be of allowing corporations the freedom to spend unlimited funds on campaign ads and how does it square with the fundamental rights of U.S. citizens? To what extent is this decision based upon an unvarnished and unrealistic interpretation of 'freedom' that privileges the corporate sector (and unions) over *individual* citizens? To what extent, for example, is there an equation between 'freedom of speech' and control of the medium of freedom of speech, or such freedom and the attention economy of voters (voting is a right of individuals not corporations)? Is the Courts' decision a vindication of the First Amendment's most basic free speech principle or does it allow corporate money to flood the political marketplace that will almost definitely corrupt democracy? In his dissenting judgment, Justice Stevens said his opposing colleagues in the majority had committed a grave error in treating corporate speech the same as that of individual human beings, and thus implying that the political process should be based on the priority of the corporate entity rather than on the individual as a logical and historical 'primitive' in the political system. The reversal certainly raises issues about the nature and future of democracy in the U.S.

Figure 10.

By overruling *Austin v. Michigan Chamber of Commerce* and striking down McCain-Feingold's ban on so-called electioneering communications, the Supreme Court has made possible the direct participation in in the U.S. political process of corporate America that allows the prospect of 'buying votes' on a massive scale. As Richard L. Hasen commented in *Slate*, echoing the opinion of many social democrats, not least Obama himself:

> It is time for everyone to drop all the talk about the Roberts court's 'judicial minimalism', with Chief Justice Roberts as an 'umpire' who just calls balls and strikes. Make no mistake, this is an activist court that is well on its way to recrafting constitutional law in its image. The best example of that is this morning's transformative opinion in *Citizens United v. FEC*. Today the court struck down decades-old limits on corporate and union spending in elections (including judicial elections) and opened up our political system to a money free-for-all (http://www.slate.com/id/2242209/).

By comparison, witness the statement by Senator Mitch McConnell (R-KY), Senate Republican Leader as reported on the CU website:

> For too long, some in this country have been deprived of full participation in the political process. With today's monumental decision, the Supreme Court took an important step in the direction of restoring the First Amendment rights of these groups by ruling that the Constitution protects their right to express themselves about political candidates and issues up until Election Day.

33

In terms of background it is interesting to note that Citizens United is a conservative organization that '*seeks to reassert the traditional American values of limited government, freedom of enterprise, strong families, and national sovereignty and security*'.[2] In law it is a 527 group designated by the Inland Revenue Service for not for profit groups that want to specifically involve themselves in political actions, elucidating the issues surrounding an individual's candidacy, or lobbying for specific laws or reforms. The website also mentions the associated American Sovereignty Project in the following terms:

> American Sovereignty Project ("ASP") is the grassroots lobbying arm of Citizens United that works to protect American sovereignty and security. ASP's major objectives include complete U.S. withdrawal from the United Nations, defeat of the treaty to establish a permanent U.N.-controlled International Criminal Court, and rejection of one-world government.

The documentary *Hillary*, a Citizens United production, produced by David Bossie, directed by Alan Peterson, written by Michael Wright and others, was funded by Lawrence Kadash and the Lincoln Club of Orange County. Lawrence Kadash as Right Web reveals, is

> a high-powered real estate investor, is a key financial backer of a number of hard-line advocacy outfits, including the Center for Security Policy and Americans for Victory over Terrorism. In 2001, Kadish was listed as one of the Republican Party's top donors, giving some $500,000 during the 2000 presidential election campaign. He is also a founding member of the Republican Jewish Coalition, which according to Mother Jones "has supported a hard-line approach to negotiating an Israeli-Palestinian peace accord, criticizing President Clinton for 'appeasing Chairman Arafat' instead of requiring 'responsibility and compliance from the Palestinian Authority'."[3]

The Lincoln Club of Orange County, founded in 1962, advertises itself as 'a cornerstone of California politics' committed 'to the principles of limited government, free enterprise, the rule of law, and the preservation of individual liberty'.[4] The club was responsible for supporting Governor Reagan's bid for power, launching Prop. 13 and the recall of Governor Gray Davis.

The film, *Hillary*,[5] is a scurrilous attack upon Hillary Clinton from the likes of right wing commentators such as Dick Morris, Ann Coulter, and Newt Gingrich, etc. Writing as early as June 18, 2007 in the U.S. Edition of *Newsweek* under the banner 'The new war on Hillary', Jonathan Darman and Mark Hosenball[6] remarked:

> Some grudges just don't die. In the 1990s, David Bossie worked tirelessly as an investigator for Rep. Dan Burton's government-reform committee. Burton was a top-echelon antagonist to Bill and Hillary Clinton, leading wide-ranging investigations of Whitewater and campaign finance. All the digging didn't amount to much: six years after the Clintons left the White House, Burton is a little-heard-from member of the minority party and Hillary Clinton is the front runner to be the Democrats' nominee for president in 2008.

Figure 11.

They continued:

> Installed in Washington, Hillary morphed into a comic-book villain for her de-
> tractors – a man-eating feminist, they claimed, who allegedly threw lamps at
> her husband, communed psychically with Eleanor Roosevelt and lit a White
> House Christmas tree adorned with sex toys. The narrative of depravity – a
> tissue of inventions by conservatives – was often hard to follow. Was she, as
> they imagined her, a secret lesbian who fostered a West Wing culture of rampant
> homosexuality? Or was she the duplicitous adulteress who slept with former law
> partner Vincent Foster, ordered his death and then made it look like a suicide?
> Disjointed as they may have been, Hillary horror tales soon became big business
> on talk radio – "That's Why the First Lady Is a Tramp" was a Clinton-era hit from
> Don Imus. In the 1996 election, a direct-mail company sold a Hillary Haters list
> with close to 30,000 names to groups advocating conservative causes.

As Matthew Mosk of the *Washington Post* reported CU wanted 'to start airing
television ads promoting the film right away. Today, the group will announce a
lawsuit it is filing against the Federal Election Commission that will try and pave
the way for Citizens United to begin running the TV ads without having to run
a disclaimer or disclose the name of the people whose donations help finance the
group's advocacy efforts'.

When Justice Kennedy wrote for a court majority of the five conservative justices, effectively he abolished any limits on the independent spending of money
in elections because it smacks of government censorship. The historic decision, a
huge win for the conservatives against Obama and potentially more serious than
the current backlash against his policies, needs to be viewed in a wider politi-

cal context over the progressive accomplishments of neoliberal readings of the economization of politics and the influence of economic readings of politics and democracy. These go back at least to Milton Friedman's 'positive economics' and Anthony Downs' (1957) *An economic theory of democracy*, that together initiated a trend that gave neoliberal economics an imperialist status against the other social sciences thus conquering the study of politics by collapsing it into economics and also helping to shape the tradition of modern public choice exemplified in James Buchanan and Gordon Tullock's (1962) *The calculus of consent: Logical foundations of constitutional democracy* which classically compared voting to a market transaction.

'Neoliberalism' is the popular label for a contemporary form of economic liberalism that cashed out itself most recently in third-generation 1960s Chicago School under Friedman, Gary Becker and Stigler and attained a 'new right' political policy formation of an alliance between conservatives and liberals under Margaret Thatcher in the British Parliament, a coalition to last for fifteen years beginning in 1979, the election of Reagan a year later in the U.S., and John Williamson's now notorious 'Washington consensus', a term he coined in 1989.[7] But it is an elusive term that elides its own contradictory historical development of the Austrian School (Carl Menger, Eugen von Böhm-Bawerk, Ludwig von Mises and Freidrich von Hayek); the German *ordoliberlen* (neoliberalism) of the Frieburg School, strongly influenced by Husserl's phenomenology, based on the Law and Economics movement by Walter Eucken, Franz Böhm, Hans Grossman-Doerth, Leonard Miksch, and practising economists Alexander Rüstow, Wilhelm Röpke, and Alfred Müller-Armack leading to Germany's and Europe's notion of the 'social market economy' (soziale Marktwirtschaft); and, the third-generation Chicago School, together with developments in public choice and constitutional economics.[8] The Austrian School, which has its origins in a subjective theory of value (sometimes known as the 'psychological' school for that reason), dates back to the late nineteenth century; the Freiburg School developed in the 1930s; the Chicago School (third-generation) develops in the early 1960s; and neoliberalism itself is a term first coined by Rüstow in 1938 but really only gained political momentum as a redefinition of classical liberalism in the 1970s, especially with the election of Margaret Thatcher and Ronald Reagan.

In her first government, Thatcher privatized many nationally-owned enterprises and sold off public housing. She reduced expenditures on social services such as education and social welfare. She attacked the unions and unemployment soared. In her second government she privatized state utilities and assets relentlessly. The economic miracle of the UK in the 1980s was not due to productivity growth but to the reduction of labor. She sold shares in a 'popular capitalism' but within a few years the ownership pattern had increased any wealth divisions. In the thirds government she introduced the dreaded 'poll tax' where, at the local level, property tax was made uniform. She privatized water, rail and electricity. British egalitarianism was at its lowest point since WWII. With privatization, the state's role to mediate the market in times of unemployment became marginalized and during her three governments so many British firms either disappeared or became foreign owned.

Figure 12.

The 1986 deregulation of the finance industry under Thatcher has been blamed for the crisis in 2008. Without doubt she marketized the British state and minimized its sphere of operations, limiting government and turning large parts of state industry over to transnational 'big' market interests.

A substantial part of the political struggle has been an argument about the role of the state; another set of political and policy arguments have concerned the coupling of political and economic systems, especially the relation of the market to democracy. William Davies reviewing Philip Mirowski and Dieter Plehwe's (2009) *The road from Mont Pèlerin: The making of the neo-liberal thought collective* and Kim Phillips-Fein's (2009) *Invisible hands: The making of the conservative movement from the new deal to Reagan*, for *Renewal* writes

> much of the history of this project confirms the suspicion, however unsophisticated, that neo-liberalism was driven by the material interests of US employers and investors. Along the way, the movement was torn between a principled, 'liberal' neo-liberalism and a capitalist, patriotic neo-liberalism. Early protagonists tended more towards the former, which they viewed as a bulwark against the threat of socialism. Yet by the 1960s, Chicago economists such as Friedman were happily promoting the interests of corporate America, with little regard for whether this actually amounted to a defence of freedom. (pp. 91–92)

Looking beyond neoliberalism Davies looks to first steps that the Left might take writing in this regard:

> The first step taken by any critic of neo-liberalism must be to disentangle the 'economic' from the 'political' once more, to resuscitate the Aristotelian sense that public discourse is a superior human capacity to private consumption. But there is risk attached to this, especially now that economic language has so suc-

cessfully infiltrated public life (think of New Labour's 'consumers' of public services). Neo-liberalism is a vicious circle of cynicism, whereby economistic depictions of politics breed hopeless, self-serving behaviour. Somehow the vicious circle must be broken, which, as Hayek knew, requires the assertion of a new intellectual paradigm altogether. (p. 92)

Davies makes a perceptive remark but how do we disentangle the economic from the political when in the name of individual freedom (with eighteenth century resonances of the founding fathers of the American constitution) the U.S. Supreme Court hands over democracy to big business, like Salome asking Herod for and getting the head of John the Baptist on a platter?

NOTES

[1] For the full Supreme Court case decision see http://supremecourtus.gov/opinions/09pdf/08-205.pdf.

[2] See the Citizens United website at http://www.citizensunited.org/index.aspx.

[3] See http://rightweb.irc-online.org/ind/kadish/kadish.html.

[4] See the website http://www.lincolnclub.org/.

[5] See the CU's promo and description of the movie, with clips, at http://www.hillarythemovie.com/.

[6] All press comment come from the CU's press site associated with the movie promo at http://www.hillarythemovie.com/press.html.

[7] Williamson himself calls it a 'damaged brandname' and itemizes it in terms of: fiscal policy discipline; redirected public spending from subsidies to infrastructure; broadening the tax base; market determined interest rates; competitive exchange rates; trade liberalization; liberalization of FDI; privatization of state assets; deregulation; and legal security for property rights. At http://www.iie.com/publications/papers/paper.cfm?researchid=486.

[8] It is roughly this analysis of economic liberalism into its three main schools that informs Michel Foucault (2008) *The birth of biopolitics*, a set of lectures he originally gave at the College de France in 1978. See also Colin Gordon's (1991) Introduction and Peters et al (2009) for a collection on 'governmentality' in education. See also Henry Giroux (2004; 2005), Peters (2001), Olssen and Peters (2007) and Roberts and Peters (2008).

REFERENCES

Buchanan, James and Tullock, Gordon (1962). *The calculus of consent: Logical foundations of constitutional democracy*.

Davies, Andrew (2009). The making of neoliberalism, *Renewal*, *17*(4), 88-92, at http://www.lwbooks.co.uk/journals/renewal/contents.html.

Downs, Anthony (1957). *An economic theory of democracy*. New York: Harper.

Foucault, Michel (2008). *The birth of biopolitics: Lectures at the College de France, 1978-1979*. Trans. Graham Burchell. New York: Palgrave Macmillan.

Giroux, Henry (2004) Neoliberalism and the Demise of Democracy: Resurrecting Hope in Dark Times, *Dissident Voice*, http://dissidentvoice.org/Aug04/Giroux0807.htm.

Giroux, Henry (Winter 2005). The terror of neoliberalism: Rethinking the significance of cultural politics, *College Literature*, *32*(1), 1-19.

Gordon, Colin (1991), Governmental rationality: An introduction. In Graham Burchell, Colin Gordon and Peter Miller (Eds), *The Foucault effect: Studies in governmentality* (pp. 1-48). Chicago, IL: University of Chicago Press.

Mirowski, Philip & Plehwe, Dieter (2009). *The road from Mont Pèlerin: The making of the neo-liberal thought collective*. New Haven: Harvard University Press.

Peters, Michael (2001). *Poststructuralism, Marxism and neoliberalism: Between theory and politics.* Lanham: Rowman & Littlefield.

Peters, Michael, Besley, T., Olssen, M., Maurer, S., & Weber, S. (2009). (Eds), *Governmentality studies in education.* Rotterdam: Sense Publishers. Foreword by Colin Gordon.

Phillips-Fein, Kim (2009). *Invisible hands: The making of the conservative movement from the new deal to Reagan.* New York: Norton.

Roberts, Peter & Peters, Michael (2008), *Neoliberalism, higher education and research.* Rotterdam: Sense.

THE GLOBAL FAILURE OF NEOLIBERALISM:
PRIVATIZE PROFITS; SOCIALIZE LOSSES

A groundswell discourse of 'the end of neoliberalism' is jamming the Left blogosphere. It has been building for some time. The Nobel prize-winning economist Joseph Stiglitz (July 7, 2008)[1] in *Project Syndicate* begins his column with the assertion that the ideology of 'market fundamentalism' has failed:

> The world has not been kind to neo-liberalism, that grab-bag of ideas based on the fundamentalist notion that markets are self-correcting, allocate resources efficiently, and serve the public interest well. It was this market fundamentalism that underlay Thatcherism, Reaganomics, and the so-called "Washington Consensus" in favor of privatization, liberalization, and independent central banks focusing single-mindedly on inflation.

Writing before the collapse of Wall Street's investment banks – the bankruptcy of Lehmann Brothers, the sell off of Merryl Lynch, the Federal bridging loan of $85 billion to AIG, and the massive $700 billion assistance to the U.S. financial sector – Stiglitz criticized neoliberal policies and their costs to developing economies.[2] He faulted the financial market allocation of resources to housing in the 1990s and the sub-prime crisis that has precipitated a global financial crisis and credit squeeze he thinks will be prolonged and widespread. He criticized the selective use of free-market rhetoric used to support special interests and the way that Bush's policies have served the military-industrial complex. He concluded:

> Neo-liberal market fundamentalism was always a political doctrine serving certain interests. It was never supported by economic theory. Nor, it should now be clear, is it supported by historical experience. Learning this lesson may be the silver lining in the cloud now hanging over the global economy.

John Quiggin (September 8, 2008),[3] the Australian social-democrat, following Stiglitz's lead and spurred by the nationalization of Fannie Mae and Freddy Mac (that between them held some $5 trillion of mortgages), under the same banner 'The End of Neoliberalism?' remarks:

> The fact that the credit crisis has reached this point marks the failure of the central claim of the neoliberal program, namely that private capital markets, free from intrusive government regulation, can enable individuals and households to handle the risks they face more flexibly and efficiently than a social-democratic welfare state.

41

Figure 13.

Others made similar claims and raised similar doubts concerning the march of neoliberalism after the Federal Reserve's bailout of Bear Stearns. Thus, Lance Freeman (18 March, 2008),[4] for instance, comments:

> The Federal Reserve's bailout (arranged liquidation to some) of Bear Stearns over the weekend seriously calls into question the headlong march toward neoliberalism that has been ascendant for the past few decades. Roughly speaking, neoliberalism called for a retrenchment of the state in favor of deregulated markets. As an ideological force neoliberalism held great sway in trade policy, the overall management of the economy and even at the local level where most planners operate.

Once a government lifeline is thrown to Wall Street the whole philosophical underpinnings of neoliberalism would have to be called into question, even among the most faithful adherents of neoliberalism. The question of government intervention becomes a matter of degree rather than kind. That is, a strong central authority is needed to guide the economy. Left to its own devices the "free market" can run off the rails. Critics of neoliberalism have pointed this out for years. But as long as most of the pain was confined to the more disadvantaged members of the world proponents of neoliberalism could wave the misfortunes off as the forces of creative destruction, etc. With the whole system under strain, that is no longer the case. The notion that reducing government and deregulation is the answer to all our problems seems laughable now.

In some sense the current series of crises that have rocked Wall Street to its foundations and threatened to destabilize the world financial system and its major banking and insurance institutions is just the latest round of failure for the global justice movement that has coordinated worldwide demonstrations against

Figure 14.

neoliberalism, 'the American imperialist project', the Iraq War, and strands referred to since the early 1980s as 'Monetarism', 'Supply-Side Economics', and
'Reaganism/Thatcherism'. Longtime critics of neoliberalism and its policies of
privatization, state non-interference and deregulation summed up in the so-called
'Washington consensus'[5] such as the economists Stiglitz, and Robert Polin (2003),
sociologist Pierre Bourdieu (1998), geographer David Harvey (2005), philoso-
pher/linguist Noam Chomsky (1999), as well as the anti-globalization movement in
general,[6] have consistently argued that neoliberalism is a class project that benefits
the rich and leads to ever-increasing inequalities both within and between states.

One of the most objectionable and inconsistent aspects of the neoliberal doctrine was the way in which market fundamentalism was *imposed* on developing
nations as part of structural adjustment loans or simply forced through political
and military measures, starting with the CIA-backed coup against a democratically
elected government in Chile in 1973 (supported strongly by Milton Friedman) and
becoming the policy stable for World Bank loans and prescriptions, especially in
Latin America during the 1980s. The imposition of market fundamentalism runs in
complete opposition to neoliberalism's own libertarian premises and emphasis on
negative freedom.

The U.S. economy's plight driven by the insurance and banking failures on Wall
Street excited the Obama–McCain debate for the U.S. presidency with McCain

Figure 15.

glossing over his support of Bush's policies and trying to play down the statement that the 'fundamentals of the economy are strong' while Obama campaigned on strengthening the economy through tax breaks to the middle classes, place emphasis on 'fair trade', and foster job creation through investment in manufacturing, and ensure protection of home ownership. The issue of the economy took pride of place in the election even dislodging the Republican emphasis on 'character' and 'leadership' that degenerated into a series of scurrilous attacks on Obama as 'terrorist', 'secret Muslim', and 'Marxist'.

The Wall Street fiasco adversely affected world stock markets in Asia, Europe and Russia (which experienced the largest one-day fall in ten years). There are network effects in terms of the global economy. Robert Reich (15 September, 2008),[7] former Secretary of Labor under Clinton, remarked that:

> Ironically, a free-market-loving Republican administration is presiding over the most ambitious intrusion of government into the market in almost anyone's memory.

And he added that although 'The sub-prime mortgage mess triggered it, but the problem lies much deeper'. He argued Wall Street is facing a crisis of trust based on promises that weren't worth the paper they were written on and he concluded:

> If what's lacking is trust rather than capital, the most important steps policymakers can take are to rebuild trust. And the best way to rebuild trust is through regulations that require financial players to stand behind their promises and tell the truth, along with strict oversight to make sure they do.

In the lead up to the last elections it seemed clear that irrespective of who would win the presidential race some major overhaul of the international financial system was (and still is) required; that government regulation must be in place, minimally, to ensure transparency and full disclosure, to spell out capital requirements and to avoid conflicts of interest; and that some new order is required with the participation of both China and India.

The move to state-centric policies and to forms of Federal regulation in the U.S. and elsewhere are now almost inevitable and many such measures are already underway. Government intervention is suddenly back in fashion and on the books at the IMF and World Bank. The move to Federal regulation and a reform of the financial system seems to chime with the development of state capitalism elsewhere, especially in East Asia,[8] and other forms of state-centrism seen as necessary for job creation and national reinvestment in infrastructure.

Immanuel Wallerstein (2008),[9] the prominent world-systems theorist, also talked of the 'demise' of neoliberalism. He explained that 'non-interference' is actually an old idea that cyclically comes into fashion and that its counterview summed up in Keynesianism (mixed economies, protection of citizens from foreign monopolies, equalization and redistribution through taxation) has also prevailed in most Western countries. He suggested that:

> The political balance is swinging back. Neoliberal globalization will be written about ten years from now as a cyclical swing in the history of the capitalist world-economy. The real question is not whether this phase is over but whether the swing back will be able, as in the past, to restore a state of relative equilibrium in the world-system. Or has too much damage been done? And are we now in for more violent chaos in the world-economy and therefore in the world-system as a whole?

As the center of economic gravity shifts to East Asia it is not clear whether new Keynesianism will be embraced or whether in face of such intensive global competition and fierce economic nationalism whether Western economies can ever afford to reestablish it. There is never the option of an innocent return historically or a return to the golden days of the welfare state in Scandinavia or New Zealand, or to the 'social model' in Europe, especially as new costly environmental and energy contingencies begin to bite. What is required is a change of *ethos* – not 'confidence' and 'trust' of the market but rather the development of trust that comes with the radically decentered democratic participation, collaboration and co-production that epitomizes the creation of public goods and distributed political, knowledge, and energy systems.

NOTES

[1] See Stiglitz's commentary at http://www.project-syndicate.org/commentary/stiglitz101.

[2] The global credit crunch started with the subprime mortgage problems in the U.S. in the three year lead-up to 2007 and the faltering of Bear Sterns which is acquired by JP Morgan Chase for $240m backed by $30b of central bank loans (March, 2008). In the UK the Government rescues Northern Rock (February, 2008) and Lloyds buys out HBOS. IMF warns that the credit crunch could be higher than 1 trillion dollars (April 2009). Indymac collapses in July and U.S. government steps in to assist Fannie Mae and Freddie Mac (guarantors of $5 trillion in mortgages) and later provides the largest

bailout in U.S. history. Major European banks falter. UK nationalizes much of its banking sector; other countries follow suit. U.S. passes $700b financial rescue plan (3rd October 2009). World stock markets experience volatility with largest ever one-day gains and losses. See the BBC credit crunch timeline: http://news.bbc.co.uk/2/hi/business/7521250.stm. World-wide network effects of credit crunch become evident, although these are not well understood by economists because of the unregulated financial derivatives and complexity of credit default-swaps. Decoupling hypothesis (e.g., China and India insulated) seems disproven. Bank of England estimates 25% decline in value of global stock markets and $2.7 trillion in credit crunch.

[3] See his blog at http://johnquiggin.com/index.php/archives/2008/09/08/the-end-of- neoliberalism/.

[4] See his blog at http://www.planetizen.com/node/30187.

[5] The original consensus was based around the following tenants: 1. Fiscal discipline; 2. Reorientation of public expenditures; 3. Tax reform; 4. Financial liberalization; 5. Unified and competitive exchange rates; 6. Trade liberalization; 7. Openness to DFI; 8. Privatization; 9. Deregulation; 10. Secure Property Rights.

[6] I take Susan George's 'A Short History of Neoliberalism' as emblematic of this movement, see http://www.zmag.org/CrisesCurEvts/Globalism/george.htm.

[7] See Robert Reich's blog at http://robertreich.blogspot.com/.

[8] In this regard see, in particular, Parag Khana's (2008), *The second world: Empires and influence in the new global order.*

[9] See Wallerstein (2008), The demise of neoliberal globalization, at http://www.monthlyreview.org/mrzine/wallerstein010208.html.

REFERENCES

Bourdieu, Pierre (March 1998). L'essence du néolibéralisme, *Le Monde diplomatique.*

Chomsky, N. (1999). *Profit over people – Neoliberalism and global order.* New York: Seven Stories Press.

Harvey, D. (2005). *A brief history of neoliberalism.* New York: Oxford University Press.

Khana, P. (2008). *The second world: Empires and influence in the new global order.* New York: Random House.

Pollin, R. (2003). *Contours of descent: U.S. economic fractures and the landscape of global austerity.* New York: Verso.

POST-AMERICANISM AND THE CHANGING ARCHITECTURE OF GLOBAL SCIENCE

The emerging political economy of global science is a significant factor influencing development of national systems of innovation, and economic, social and cultural development, with the rise of multinational actors and a new mix of corporate, private/public and community involvement. It is only since the 1960s with the development of research evaluation and increasing sophistication of bibliometrics that it has been possible to map the emerging economy of global science, at least on a comparative national and continental basis. The Science Citation Index provides bibliographic and citational information from 3,700 of the world's scientific and technical journals covering over one hundred disciplines. The expanded index available in an online version covers more than 5,800 journals. Comparable 'products' in the social sciences (SSCI) and humanities (A&HCI) cover, respectively, bibliographic information from 1,700 journals in 50 disciplines and 1,130 journals.

On a world scale it is now possible to get some idea of science distributions in terms of academic papers for the first time. An issue of the UIS Bulletin on Science and Technology Statistics (UNESCO 2005), published in collaboration with the *Institut National de la Recherche Scientifique* (INRS) (Montréal, Canada), presents a bibliometric analysis of 20 years of world scientific production (1981-2000), as reflected by the publications indexed in the Science Citation Index (SCI). It indicates that:

> In 2000 the SCI included a total of 584,982 papers, representing a 57.5% increase from 1981, when 371,346 papers were published worldwide. Authors with addresses in developed countries wrote 87.9% of the papers in 2000, a decrease from 93.6% in 1981. Developing countries, on the other hand, saw a steady increase in their share of scientific production: from 7.5% of world papers in 1981 to 17.1% in 2000 ... Since 1981 the world map of publications changed significantly. North America lost the lead it had in 1996, and in 2000 produced 36.8% of the world total, a decrease from 41.4% in 1981. The opposite trend can be found in the European Union, which in 2000 published 40.2% of the world total, up from 32.8% in 1981. Japan went up from 6.9% to 10.7% in 2000. Collectively this 'triad' has therefore maintained its dominance, accounting for 81% of the world total of scientific publications in 2000, up from 72% in 1981.

While sub-Saharan African publications remained stable at around 1% of the world total, and the share of publications from the Arab States increased from 0.6% in

1981 to 0.9% in 2000, and the Central Eastern European share remained stable around 3% of the world total, both the Newly-Industrialised Countries (NIC) in Asia (a group that includes China) and Latin America and the Caribbean (LAC) increased their share significantly, respectively, from 0.6% of the world total in 1981 to 4.2% in 2000 (with China accounting for 85% of the publications an increase from 63% in 1981), and 1.3% to 3.2% in LAC countries. The SCI covers biology, biomedicine, chemistry, clinical medicine, earth and space, engineering and technology, mathematics, and physics.

The UIS Bulletin concludes that the developed world share of publications has declined while developing regions (Asia and Latin America) have expanded and Africa has stagnated. There is also clear evidence that there has been considerable growth in international collaboration. These bibliometric measures present a biased view in the sense that they do not take into account book citations, important for the humanities and social sciences, and they tend to favor English as the global medium of communication. Nevertheless, used with caution, as the UNESCO publication suggests, they can reveal some insights through trends regarding aspects of scientific production at global level.

Britain's Chief Scientist David A. King (2004) provides an analysis of the output and outcomes from research investment over the past decade, to measure the quality of research on national scales and to set it in an international context, reveals the unevenness of world distribution of science and ascendancy of a group of 31 countries[1] that accounted for 'more than 98% of the world's highly cited papers, defined by Thomson ISI as the most cited 1% by field and year of publication. The world's remaining 162 countries contributed less than 2% in total' (p. 311). His analysis reveals the overwhelming dominance of the United States, whose share has declined recently, United Kingdom and Germany, and the fact that 'The nations with the most citations are pulling away from the rest of the world' (p. 311). He provides the following analysis:

> The countries occupying the top eight places in the science citation rank order … produced about 84.5% of the top 1% most cited publications between 1993 and 2001. The next nine countries produced 13%, and the final group share 2.5%. There is a stark disparity between the first and second divisions in the scientific impact of nations. Moreover, although my analysis includes only 31 of the world's 193 countries, these produce 97.5% of the world's most cited papers. (p. 314)

And King goes on to draw the following conclusion:

> The political implications of this last comparison are difficult to exaggerate. South Africa, at 29th place in my rank ordering, is the only African country on the list. The Islamic countries are only represented by Iran at 30th, despite the high GDP of many of them and the prominence of some individuals, such as Nobel prizewinners Abdus Salam (physics, 1979) and Ahmed Zewail (chemistry, 1999). (p. 314)

There are clear signs that architecture of global science is shifting especially with the huge investment in research and the consequent growth of scientific publica-

Figure 16.

tions in Asia. Adams and Wilsdon (2006) report that China's spending on research has increased by more than 20% per year, reaching 1.3% of GDP in 2005 and making it third in the global league table in research expenditure after U.S. and Japan. Science budgets in India have increased by the same annual percentage, adding some 2.5 million IT, engineering and life sciences graduates, 650,000, postgraduates and 6,000 PhDs every year.

The U.S. National Science Board's (2008) publication *Research and development: Essential foundation for U.S. competiveness in a global economy* charts the decline since 2005 of Federal and industry support for basic research which accounted for 18% ($62B) of the $340B U.S research budget in current dollars in 2006. The report comments:

> Federal obligations for academic research (both basic and applied) and especially in the current support for National Institutes of Health (NIH) (whose budget had previously doubled between the years 1998 to 2003) declined in real terms between 2004 and 2005 and are expected to decline further in 2006 and 2007. This is the first multiyear decline in Federal obligations for academic research since 1982.

The report also clearly shows the declining competiveness of U.S. science and technology: patents dropped from 55% of world total in 1996 to 53% in 2005; and basic research articles published in peer-reviewed journals by authors from U.S. private industry peaked in 1995 and declined by 30% between 1995 and 2005. The report goes on to say: 'The drop in physics publications was particularly dramatic: decreasing from nearly 1,000 publications in 1988 to 300 in 2005'. The loss in U.S. share and its decline of science and technology 'reflects the rapid rise in share by the East Asia-4 (comprising China, South Korea, Singapore, and Taiwan)'. The architecture of world science is changing rapidly. The U.S. needs a comprehensive strategy based on an understanding of the globalization of science, the promotion of innovation through international collaboration and the global value chain if it is to remain competitive in the coming decades.

NOTES

[1] The countries are: *Australia*, Austria, Belgium, *Brazil*, *Canada*, *China*, Denmark, Finland, *France*, *Germany*, Greece, *India*, Iran, Ireland, Israel, *Italy*, *Japan*, Luxembourg, the Netherlands, Poland, Portugal, *Russia*, Singapore, Spain, *South Africa*, *South Korea*, Sweden, Switzerland, Taiwan, the *United Kingdom* and the *United States* (with G20 countries, excluding European only members, in italics).

REFERENCES

Adams, J. & Wilsdon, J. (2006). *The new geography of science: UK research and international collaboration.* London: Demos.

King, D.A. (15 July 2004). The scientific impact of nations: What different countries get for their research spending, *Nature, 430,* 311-316, at www.nature.com/nature.

National Science Board (2008). *Research and Development: Essential Foundation for U.S. Competiveness in a Global Economy,* at http://www.nsf.gov/statistics/nsb0803/start.htm.

UNESCO (2005). What do bibliometric indicators tell us about world scientific output? *UIS Bulletin on Science and Technology Statistics, 2,* September.

CHAPTER 7

ECOPOLITICS OF 'GREEN ECONOMY', ENVIRONMENTALISM AND EDUCATION

(with Rodrigo Britez)

INTRODUCTION

The 'green economy' has emerged as a strong policy direction in Obama's administration with $100 billion in dedicated funds over the next decade to provide infrastructure investment for a range of initiatives including alternative energy technologies that will lessen the reliance on foreign oil supplies. The concept of the 'green economy' has appeared at the point of the collapse of neoliberal ideology of deregulation and a new age of poverty after the worst global recession since WWII. First, this chapter reviews the claims of 'green capitalism' examining, in particular, the promise of distributed energy systems and the 'hydrogen economy' as proposed solutions to the energy problem of the U.S. economy. Second, it proposes a postmodern critique of neoliberal economics before examining conceptions of the green economy and its sustainability. The chapter concludes by looking more broadly at the need for a broad shift from anthropocentric conceptions of economy to one based on a systems framework, and in this light, considers the relations among ecopolitics, environmental education and prospects for green capitalism.

GREEN ECONOMY: THE NEW POLICY AGENDA

The ideology of neoliberalism is in tatters and the free market belief system based on privatization and deregulation is in disrepute. The global economic and financial crisis sparked by the U.S. subprime collapse in the housing market and the associated credit squeeze have destabilized the world economy and vindicated those who criticized neoliberal policies as unsustainable. As a consequence the world is facing the worst global economic, financial and social crisis since the Great Depression. It is estimated that some $35 trillion in assets has been lost or wiped off national accounts. Globally, we face a *new age of poverty* with rising unemployment in both the developing and developed worlds and a huge increase in numbers living on less than two dollars a day. At the same time the planet Earth faces multiple environmental crises including those of climate change, dwindling carbon-based energy resources, food security, and increasingly polluted water and air. In this chaotic environment policy-makers and politicians are launching programs that emphasize sustainability and attempt to build on the promise and prospect of the 'green economy'.

51

Figure 17.

Barack Obama has made it clear that he sees a direct link between America's strategic and long term economic interests, climate change and renewable and clean energy technologies. In his first budget he allocated over $100 billion in green investments in energy efficient buildings, alternative energy technologies and better, more effective forms of public transport. He and his team have also devoted resources to a re-tooled, re-imagined auto industry and are calling on Congress to cut carbon emissions. Part of Obama's election plan was to create 5 million 'green' jobs in a decade. It is also clear that there has been a 'greening' of the massive stimulus package.

Brussels and the EU also have been touting the 'green economy' building it into the Lisbon agenda and targeting Europe to become a leader in green-innovation. Major are also caught up in this new shift: oil companies define themselves as 'energy companies of tomorrow', and every industry from auto-makers to fast-food to fashion are painting themselves as green and sustainable. Climate change industries and alternative energy technologies combined now match software and biotech industries and some argue that the world is on the edge of a new 'Kondratiev' wave of economic development – the age of sustainability and renewal resources based on an 'economics of abundance'.

The United Nations Environmental Program launched its Green Economy Initiative (GEI) in October, 2008 aimed growing the green shoots of tomorrow's economy. *A global green new deal* (UNEP, 2009) prepared by Edward B. Barbier from the Department of Economics & Finance at the University of Wyoming, suggests that out of crisis we face a global opportunity to launch a 'Global Green New Deal' (GGND) as the right mix of policies that can encourage recovery, growth and sustainability. The report argues we can not simply expect to resume business-as-usual. We need to embrace the three objectives of a GGND: revive the world economy, create employment opportunities and protect vulnerable groups; reduce carbon dependency, ecosystem degradation and water scarcity, and further the Millennium Development Goal of ending extreme world poverty by 2015. The report highlights the economic and employment implications of greening the energy sector including the alleged fact that 'Green energy initiatives have the potential to save the U.S. economy an average of US$450 million per year for every US$1 billion invested' and that 'the renewable energy sector of China has a value of nearly US$17 billion and already employs close to 1 million workers' (p. 10). Low-carbon transport strategies can also stimulate growth and create jobs and 'There is a link between reducing ecological scarcity and improving the livelihoods of the poor' (p. 11).

Despite efforts over the past decades to demonstrate the inter-dependency between the environment and human well-being, the environment continues to receive marginal attention in economic policymaking. Worldwide, billions of dollars are spent annually to subsidise carbon-emitting fossil fuels. Meanwhile, investment in renewable energy remains inadequate, posing a threat to affordable and secure energy supply. Investment in the agricultural sector including water and soil conservation has actually declined in the last ten years in the developing world, threatening food security when the world's major food producers are subsidised to turn food into biofuels.

This continued environmental neglect is due to the lack of a powerful economic case for investing in the environment. The Green Economy Initiative will make that economic case while providing policymakers and other stakeholders with information on the important role of the government in the march towards a green economy. In addition, the report will prove that environmental areas such as ecosystems, clean and efficient technology, renewable energy, chemical and waste management, biodiversity based business, and sustainable cities, buildings, construction, and transport are the new engines for economic growth in the future. It will argue that investing in these sectors can contribute to rapid economic recovery in the short term and sustained economic growth over the next few decades with positive contributions to decent job creation and poverty reduction.

This chapter first reviews the claims of 'green capitalism' examining, in particular the promise of distributed energy systems and the 'hydrogen economy' as solutions in part to the energy problem of the U.S. economy. The next section proposes a postmodern critique of neoliberal economics before examining conceptions of the green economy and its sustainability. The paper concludes by looking more broadly at the need for a broad shift from anthropocentric conceptions of economy to one based on a systems framework, and finally, in this light, considers the relations among ecopolitics, environmental education and green capitalism.

GREEN CAPITALISM AND DISTRIBUTED ENERGY SYSTEMS

The current crisis of the U.S. economy brings together a number of related problems that pose a deepening and complex problem and has led a number of commentators to predict the end of American hegemony and world power. The latest is Fareed Zakaria's (2008a) analysis that indicates the end of 'Pax Americana': 'The world has shifted from anti-Americanism to *post*-Americanism'. Zakaria argues:

Figure 18.

We are living through the third great power shift in modern history. The first was the rise of the Western world, around the 15th century. It produced the world as we know it now – science and technology, commerce and capitalism, the industrial and agricultural revolutions. It also led to the prolonged political dominance of the nations of the Western world. The second shift, which took place in the closing years of the 19th century, was the rise of the United States. Once it industrialized, it soon became the most powerful nation in the world, stronger than any likely combination of other nations. For the last 20 years, America's superpower status in every realm has been largely unchallenged – something that's never happened before in history, at least since the Roman Empire dominated the known world 2,000 years ago. During this Pax Americana, the global economy has accelerated dramatically. And that expansion is the driver behind the third great power shift of the modern age – the rise of the rest.[1]

According to Zakaria, Americans should not be worried because a post-American world 'will not be a world defined by the decline of America but rather the rise of everyone else. It is the result of a series of positive trends that have been progressing over the last 20 years, trends that have created an international climate of unprecedented peace and prosperity'. Zakaria's polite and optimistic analysis focuses on the economic expansion that allegedly comes with globalization that accounts for the growth in economic power of China, India, Brazil and Russia. But economic growth is not a zero sum game: America benefits from the 'rise of the rest'. And the openness and flexibility of U.S. society means that it will adapt in an ultimately win-win scenario. One of the problems is that economic and political power to a very large extent requires and reinforces one another and that world politics is a zero sum game. Inevitably, American political power will decline as other world powers gain greater economic and therefore political power. We have already seen some of the signs of this change in the template of world politics with China's massive infrastructure investment in Africa, especially in the oil producers (Nigeria, Angola, Sudan, Equatorial Guinea, Gabon, Republic of Congo), the rise of Middle-Eastern oil-rich States with their huge sovereign wealth funds, the new found wealth of Russia that has allowed it to flex its foreign policy muscles (a huge turnaround since the so-called end of the Cold War), the further enlargement and integration of the EU, and the rise of the Asian tiger economies.

Zakaria's analysis gives the U.S. a false comfort zone and also fails to take account of the complexity of the economic situation and its long term consequences. There are at least five aspects of the current economic crisis that indicates a complexity and deepening of the problem not fully understood or realized by many analysts and pundits.

— the collapse of the subprime housing market bubble that has reportedly caused over two million foreclosures and spread to the real estate housing market and the building industry;
— the U.S.-led credit crunch and ongoing international financial crisis with massive writedowns and losses by banks and securities firms totaling more than $1 trillion dollars, according to the IMF's annual Global Financial Stability report released April 8 2008;
— the energy crisis and specifically a series of oil price hikes that pushed the price to over $130 a barrel and $4 per gallon at the pump with huge effects on consumers and the U.S. automobile industry;
— a $3 trillion Iraq war after five years (Stiglitz, 2008) including death benefits, that represents opportunity cost investment in U.S. infrastructure, health and education;
— finally, the declining power of the U.S. dollar with collapsing trade balances and a yawning current account deficit.

Taken together this complex of problems represents an irreversible change, especially since oil as a resource is limited or fixed and demand for it is driven by the demand from a voracious Chinese economy growing at over 10% per year and accounting for a large proportion of the world oil market. It is ironic that George W. Bush, the second oil President, may have hastened America's decline but he did not cause it. One could also argue that the prevailing neoliberal ideology of the unregulated free market has once again made 'market failure' a respectable topic, with talk from both Bernanke and Paulson about reforming the credit market and lending rules as well as new intergovernmental efforts to examine and regulate the world finance industry. And yet at least one element – the energy crisis – in this complex may be a blessing in disguise for the U.S. but may, at the same time, point to yet another bubble based on alternative energy and green capitalism.

In *The hydrogen economy* (2003), best-selling author Jeremy Rifkin takes us on an eye-opening journey into the next great commercial era in history. He envisions the dawn of a new economy powered by hydrogen that will fundamentally change the nature of our market, political and social institutions, just as coal and steam power did at the beginning of the industrial age. Rifkin observes that we are fast approaching a critical watershed for the fossil-fuel era, with potentially dire consequences for industrial civilization. While experts had been saying that we had another forty or so years of cheap available crude oil left, some of the world's leading petroleum geologists are now suggesting that global oil production could peak and begin a steep decline much sooner, as early as the end of this decade. Non-OPEC oil producing countries are already nearing their peak production, leaving most of the remaining reserves in the politically unstable Middle East. Increasing tensions between Islam and the West are likely to further threaten our access to affordable oil. In desperation, the U.S. and other nations could turn to dirtier fossil-fuels – coal, tar sand, and heavy oil – which will only worsen global warming and imperil the earth's already beleaguered ecosystems. Looming oil shortages make industrial life vulnerable to massive disruptions and possibly even collapse.

While the fossil-fuel era is entering its sunset years, a new energy regime is being born that has the potential to remake civilization along radical new lines, according to Rifkin. Hydrogen is the most basic and ubiquitous element in the universe. It is the stuff of the stars and of our sun and, when properly harnessed, it is the 'forever fuel'. It never runs out and produces no harmful CO^2 emissions.

Commercial fuel-cells powered by hydrogen are just now being introduced into the market for home, office and industrial use. The major automakers have spent more than two billion dollars developing hydrogen cars, buses, and trucks, and the first mass-produced vehicles are expected to be on the road in just a few years.

The hydrogen economy makes possible a vast redistribution of power, with far-reaching consequences for society. Today's centralized, top-down flow of energy, controlled by global oil companies and utilities, becomes obsolete. In the new era, says Rifkin, every human being could become the producer as well as the consumer of his or her own energy – so called 'distributed generation'. When millions of end-users connect their fuel-cells into local, regional, and national hydrogen energy webs (HEWs), using the same design principles and smart technologies that made possible the World Wide Web, they can begin to share energy – peer-to-peer – creating a new decentralized form of energy use.

Hydrogen has the potential to end the world's reliance on imported oil and help diffuse the dangerous geopolitical game being played out between Muslim militants and Western nations. It will dramatically cut down on carbon dioxide emissions and mitigate the effects of global warming. And because hydrogen is so plentiful and exists everywhere on earth, every human being could be 'empowered', making it the first truly democratic energy regime in history.

THE POSTMODERN CRITIQUE OF NEOLIBERAL ECONOMICS

The postmodern critique is not merely a negative account of neoclassical assumptions or simply an updating of economics according to the debates of the 1980s and after. It also constitutes a positive moment that provides important directions for the future. I have called these directions the 'greening the knowledge economy' by which I mean a constellation after the 'second industrial divide' of a synergistic relation between two mega-trends, imperatives and forces that acting upon one another become a significant trajectory for postindustrial economies. The tradition of economics of information and knowledge now is a well documented field that coalesces with other disciplines to define the discourse of the knowledge economy (Peters & Besley, 2006; Peters, 2008). This discourse both predates and postdates neoliberalism although it has also been given a neoliberal reading by world policy agencies like the World Bank based on a version of human capital theory with investment in key competencies, and neoliberal restructuring of education based on principles of deregulation, privatization and the introduction of student loans.

The neoliberal reading is also sometimes associated with the growth of sign economies and financialization of the global economy (Forster, 2007). Yet the neoliberal reading is only one reading and it does not analyze or identify the notion of knowledge as a global public good that demands government intervention designed to protect the public domain. The neoliberal reading does not take into account or try to explain the fundamental differences between the traditional industrial economy and the knowledge economy except by reference to pure rationality assumptions that do not sit well or apply within networked environments or merging distributive knowledge ecologies. In these 'ecological' environments none of the elements of homo economicus focusing on individuality, rationality and self-interest apply. The neoliberal reading does not understand how knowledge as a commodity behaves differently from other commodities. Neither does it recognize the parallel discourse of the 'knowledge society' that begins in the sociological literature on postindustrialism in the early 1960s which is often directed at concerns about new forms of stratification, universal access to knowledge and the role and significance of knowledge workers and institutions (Peters & Besley, 2006). Finally, the neoliberal reading is stuck temporally in the 1990s and does not take account of the movement towards various forms of the open economy signified in the creative economy, the learning economy, and the open science economy (see Peters, 2009a, b).

CONCEPTIONS OF THE GREEN ECONOMY

Perhaps most importantly the neoliberal reading does not recognize the way in which conceptions of the green economy now offer both new strategic and policy directions in ways that reinforce and interact dynamically with the knowledge economy.[2] Brian Milani (2000), for instance, in his Designing the Green Economy: *The postindustrial alternative to corporate globalization* argues that the ecological economy is an authentic postindustrialism based on principles of regeneration and sustainability aimed at quality of life, community rebuilding and environmental renewal. The green economy is based on the recognition of ecological principles of self-organization, protection of diversity, and the enhancement of network flows.[3]

Neoclassical economics based on rationalistic and reductionist assumptions does not have the conceptual or philosophical resources to recognize the significance of natural assets, their relational contexts and their renewable and dynamic environments that presupposed elements of the ecosystem: throughput, distributive development, feedback and scale (see Daly, 2003). Founded on the work of Kenneth E. Boulding (1978), Nicholas Georgescu-Roegen's bioeconomics (1971; see also Mayumi, 2001), and Hermann Daly (1999) ecological economics addresses the interdependence of human economies and natural ecosystems and has strong connections with both green economics and ecology with the focus on networks.[4]

IS SUSTAINABLE CAPITALISM POSSIBLE?

An additional question is if a green economy is viable within the frame of a capitalist society and economy. The ambiguous term 'green' economy can contain multiple meanings. It may imply the emergence of more sustainable ways of global consumption and production, but at the same time it can be used as an empty rhetoric device apply in the developed industrial world to justify the continuity of the political primacy of certain countries and geographic locations within the global capitalist political economic system.

More important, the idea of 'green' economy as equivalent to sustainable forms of capitalism is still open to question. The main crux is about the ecological sustainability of capitalism itself as economic system confronted with the limits of a looming biocrisis does not necessarily have a positive answer.

James O'Connor (1993) indicates that the answer to this question is probably 'no'. He points out that one of the basic conditions to begin to think on ecological sustainable forms of capitalist production require a deep social and political commitment to protect the threaten biodiversity. Instead, the use of the level 'green' in green capitalism, as in the case of sustainable development, may imply the emergence of new corporate practices, through their research and development departments, attempting to 'reform and restructure nature to make it consistent with profitable accumulation – e.g. plantation, forestry, biotechnological agriculture' (p. 126).

Resources are constructed, but if we assume that natural biodiversity is not renewable, then there are three basic arguments that support an assertion contrary to the possibility of finding a solution to the current ecological crisis within Capitalism 2.0. First, the economy of abundance that is deemed possible within the knowledge sectors is confronted with an economy of limited resources in terms of natural biodiversity and ecologies. The basic problem confronted is the commoditization of nature and human beings that capitalist growth requires. Precisely, John Ikerd (2005) points out, 'capitalistic economies inherently are extractive, with respect to the natural resources upon which they must depend for productivity and are exploitative, with respect to the societies within which they function' (p. 1). It adjusts to demands for improvements of ecological, as well as social balance, usually through social pressures and public policies. In those instances, it is very difficult to considering a greening of capitalism at a global scale without the intermingling of both social justice and ecological integrity.

These elements are generally diffused or ignored in the discourses of corporate and policy leaders in relation to 'green' initiatives. Second, the term 'green' is many times used merely a byword of sustainable development, and a rather sound rhetorical advertisement when applied in reference to the developing world. Bill Willers (1994) points out that the term sustainable development first appeared in 1987 after the United Nations' Bruntland report. The report itself is important because it identifies a definition of sustainable development that shares aspects of the current discussion on the possibility of a green economy within capitalism.

According to this report's definition, sustainable development is 'development that meets the needs of the present without missing the ability of future generations to meet their own needs' (Brundtland, 1987). But, as Willers (1994) cleverly indicates, the word itself is in fact used as 'code for perpetual growth' (p. 1146).

In the same way that the current discourse about a green economy promises the emergence of a new set of 'green' industries, the idea of sustainable development that was used in the 1980s indicated a global project that requires the need for increasing the manufacturing input, rather than practicing the idea of 'respecting environmental constrains' (Willers 1994, p. 1146). In those terms the term 'green' economy may very well become another 'world deception', especially if this does not contain a debate about the problem of the ecological limits of economic growth in the context of a planetary ecosystem threaten with a wave of mass extinction. A knowledge economy can be an economy of boundless resources and growth, but growth, or more precisely capitalist growth itself as 'long ago became the enemy of the natural world' (Willers, 1994, p. 1148).

Third, contemporary green capitalist advocates and entrepreneurs still seem deluded with the idea that technology, as in new forms of clean energy, by itself is a solution for the current ecological problems and contradictions generated within capitalist economies.

The idea is that 'green technologies', green industries and the market will be able to partly solve the contradictions of the compound social and ecological crisis that results from following the logic of growth, accumulation and consumption prevalent at capitalist economies. Basically, they propose a what York, Clark and Foster (2009) announce as a 'technological wonderland' that assumes that the current crisis 'mostly comes down to energy efficiency (and other technical fixes) without understanding that in a capitalist system, growth of efficiency normally leads to an increase in scale of the economy (and furthers rifts in ecological systems that more than negates any ecological gains made (a problem known as Jevons Paradox)'.

The interesting point of this argument is not that we are confronting eco-scarcity, because contrary to the majority of environmental discourses the environment does not have finite and impermanent resources when viewed through. Oil can be replaced by hydrogen cells, natural seeds are replaced with bio-engineered seeds. However, the natural biodiversity of the environment, once lost, cannot be renewed.

There are losers and winners in these processes of capitalist development. We cannot replace the species lost in the current wave of mass extinction. Even if we acquired in the future the technological capacity of cloning some of then, is difficult to consider that we will be able to replace the lost balance of their environments that often includes human ecologies. For example, practice of intensive industrial agriculture, that relied on deforestation, often leads to the lost of productive land. This has short term economic benefits, but also ecological and human consequences for local communities.

Infinite energy resources are not the answer to the loss of nature's diversity or the ecological and social consequences that ecological disruption generates. The massive displacement of populations has been only one of them. In fact it only answers the crisis of the economic system, rather than questions about the possibility of ecological sustainability of the economy or on ways to deal with human consequences that the loss of those ecologies and the consequent ecological disruptions produce.

Jevon's paradox (Alcott, 2005), was stated by William Stanley Jevons in the 19th century in his book *The coal question*. Jevon's paradox is used by ecological economics literature to challenge 'the pervasive assumption ... that sustainability emerges as a passive consequence of consuming less' the optimistic version of this assumption considers that technological innovation, as in the case of the informational technology revolution, 'will reduce our consumption of resources to such an extent that we will become sustainable without requiring people to sacrifice the things that the enjoy' (Mayumi, Giampietro & Alcott, 2008, p. x). On the contrary, Jevon's paradox points out that technological innovation fosters greater levels of consumption, thus non-renewable resources became less sustainable. Improvements in efficiency, in capitalist economies generate more consumption. For example, as with oil or any other non-renewable resource, 'growth, both of populations and of economies, undermines future sustainability because new technologies have not in fact decreased per capita dependence upon finite resources' (Hall, 2006, p. 89).

Today, a possible answer to the Jevon's paradox could be forms of global public action and regulation of these finite resources. However, this is difficult to reconcile within the tenets of the logic of profit and theory of economic growth and consumption dominant in capitalist economies. At the same time, a viable green economy seems to require local initiatives placing the social at center of economic planning. This seems contradictory with the tenets of for profit oriented economies as conceived by neo-liberal ideologies. The provision of basic human needs for the population is often ignored in the discussions about the market and green capitalism. However, it is not possible to conceive forms of ecopolitics without addressing social injustices and the central place that human beings as part of the environment play. For example, is very difficult to conceive a solution to the problems of pollution in mega cities in the global south while ignoring the populations of their slumps and shanty towns. In the same way, it is not possible to conceive forms of viable ecological sustainability while ignoring the specific needs of the human populations that are part of the environment. The basic problem is that those needs are set under the parameters of a system of economic growth and consumption which are based in the non-sustainability of natural environments.

The answer of the new green global policy agenda seems very precise. In absence of non-renewable natural biodiversity, corporate global companies' and countries' policy actions indicated so far, and for the most part are a trajectory of initiatives to accommodate nature to the purposes of a capitalist economy rather than to the urgency of finding a sustainable ecological balance between environment and economic activity. A larger consideration seems now that in capitalist economies, human activity and technological innovations will be able to effectively address the loss of natural ecologies, and more importantly, deal with the humanistic and ecological crises and consequences that this loss undoubtedly generates. The question that has to be asked is whether sustainability is possible within a market society, or whether green capitalism is possible at all? The assessment of this question involves the idea that there are different forms of market society (and different forms of capitalism) that in part are created by the legal-juridical rules passed and enacted by governments. It is clearly not the case that industrial socialism fares any better, and any kind of industrialism, especially that based on extractive industries, quickly reaches environmental limits.

The notion that there are forms of postindustrialist (either capitalist or socialist) knowledge based industries (perhaps systems of open knowledge production) that are inherently clean (or less damaging to the environment) or smart and/or promote a new dynamic ecological relationship with the environment, has yet to be fully assessed. These claims might be overstated however, that also that investment in renewable and alternative energy forms is a constructive move, especially if the new clean, green, smart energy technologies are distributive technologies, i.e., systems that the individual (pro)sumer can tap into and co-deign, co-create. There are already some examples not restricted to energy-saving technologies.

FROM ANTHROPOCENTRISM TO SYSTEMS[5]

As the renowned theoretical physicist Stephen Hawking indicates in a lecture *On the beginning of time*, 'All the evidence seems to indicate, that the universe has not existed forever, but that it had a beginning, about 15 billion years ago. This is probably the most remarkable discovery of modern cosmology. Yet it is now taken for granted'.[6] He outlines how the discussion whether or not the universe had a beginning persisted through the 19th and 20th centuries and was conducted on the basis of theology, philosophy and on the basis of anthropocentric assumptions with little consideration of observational evidence, partly because of the unreliability of cosmological evidence up until very recently. 'Big Bang', the name for a cosmological model of the universe coined by Fred Hoyle for a theory he did not believe, began with observations by Edwin Hubble and his discovery of evidence for the continuous expansion of the universe. In essence, the theory is based notably on observations of the Cosmic Microwave Background Radiation, large-scale structures, and the redshifts of distant supernovae (see Ross, 2008). The technical details need not detain us here as there are many good accounts of the standard model. What is important for our purposes is to note the shift from a set of anthropocentric assumptions to a theory based on observation and its importance for providing an observational and empirical basis for an environmental ethics based on the existence, life, scale and longevity of the sun at the centre of our solar system. This feature requires some comment because it is an unusual claim to consider the way in which empirical matters to some extent determine the philosophical nature of environmental ethics even where the notion of ethics in relation to the environment is also unclear. Yet it seems clear that environmental ethics as the theory of environmental right conduct or the environmental good life (where the notion of life itself is, definitionally, at stake) rests fundamentally upon the notion of 'environment' and how we understand it.

Environmental ethics has been slow to develop and has suffered from anthropocentrism or 'human-centeredness' embedded in traditional western ethical thinking that has assigned intrinsic value only to human beings considered as separate moral entities from their supporting environment. The difficulty is whether such anthropocentric accounts can re-conceive the relations between human beings and their environment and if so, whether the concept of environment might be taken in an extra-terrestrial sense as applying to our solar system with the sun at the centre. This seems more like the environmental package that has a kind of systemic wholeness and integrity as a system with the energy source at its center without which life would not be possible.

If we are to accept this more inclusive notion of environment that decenters Earth within the solar system, then the notion of environment has to be renegotiated as one that dynamically also includes the lifespan of the solar system. One of the advantages of this definitional move is to resituate human beings in relation to the 'environment' out of which they emerged in a number of evolutionary steps towards complex intelligent life forms and systems, and into which they will finally remerged. When environmental ethics emerged in the 1970s it began to call for a change of values based on ecological understandings that emphasized the interconnectivity of all life and thereby issued a challenge to theological, philosophical and scientific accounts that posited individual moral agents as separate from, and logically prior to, their environment. This challenge drew on early environmental studies, and prompted the emergence of ecology as a formal discipline, and deep ecology, as well as feminist, new animism, and later social ecology and bioregional accounts, sought to dislodge anthropocentric accounts that gave intrinsic value to human beings at the expense of the moral value of living systems (Brenan & Lo, 2008). While this insight does not establish what kind of environmental ethical theory one should adopt it does establish the prima facie case that traditional theories of ethics have been unable to talk about the environment in ethical terms. This is largely because they have been bolstered by deep anthropocentric assumptions that are embedded in earlier modern, scientific accounts of 'nature', and also in the nature of industrial capitalism (White, 1967; Merchant, 1990).

ECOPOLITICS, ENVIRONMENTAL EDUCATION AND GREEN CAPITALISM

Ecopolitics must come to terms with the scramble for resources that increasingly dominate the competitive motivations and long range resource planning of the major industrial world powers. There are a myriad of new threats to the environment that have been successfully spelled out by eco-philosophers that have already begun to impact upon the world in all their facets. First, there is the depletion of non-renewable resources and, in particular, oil, gas, rainforest timber and minerals. Second, and in related-fashion, is the energy crisis itself upon which the rapidly industrializing countries and the developed world depend. Third, is the rise of China and India with their prodigious appetites that will match the U.S. within a few decades in a rapacious demand for more of everything that in turn triggers resource scrambles and the heavy investment in resource-rich regions such as Africa. Fourth, global climate change will have the greatest impact upon the world's poorest countries, multiplying the risk of conflict and resource wars. With these trends and possible scenarios only a better understanding of the environment can save us and the planet. A better understanding of the earth's environmental system is essential if scientists in concert with politicians, policy-makers and business leaders are to promote green exchange and to ascertain whether green capitalism strategies that aim at long-term sustainability are possible.

The energy crisis may be a blessing in disguise for the U.S. Jeremy Rifkin (2003) envisions a new economy powered by hydrogen that will fundamentally change the nature of our market, political and social institutions as we approach the end of the fossil-fuel era, with inescapable consequences for industrial society. New hydrogen fuel-cells are now being pioneered which together with the design principles of smart information technologies can provide new distributed forms of energy use. Thomas Friedman (2008) also argues the crisis can lead to reinvestment in infrastructure and alternative energy sources in the cause of nation-building. Education has an important role to play in the new energy economy both in terms of changing worldview and the promotion of a green economy but also in terms of research and development's contribution to energy efficiency, battery storage and new forms of renewable energy.

At this stage of the world's development, with space travel, planetary exploration, satellite communications systems in space, and scientific probing of the beginnings of the universe, the concept of environment itself needs radical extension to the solar system and universe. Increasingly, although it is still early days, the earth needs to be thought of not just as Gaia, as an organic living system, but also as part of a larger, more broadly embracing environmental system. The notion that the environment is a dynamic concept, of which we are a part, is the central understanding of a greening of capitalism. Sustainable prosperity becomes possible with a shift to knowledge and creative economies based on services and clean, efficient technologies, although the ecological society depends on a broad consensus over the nature of the market and the economic system: What are the conflicts between the market and ecological economics? (Daly & Farley, 2004). Does sustainability imply 'limits' and to what extent? (Greenwood, 2007). Can Green Capitalism 2.0

solve the looming biocrisis within the constraints of a green mixed economy? 'Natural capital', the self-renewing eco-system on which all wealth depends, is the basis of green capitalism and we need to develop democratic and participatory means by which to encourage and pursue it. This is one of the great tasks facing education at all levels in the 21st century.

NOTES

[1] This excerpt is taken from Zakaria's (2008b), The rise of the rest, appearing in *Newsweek* at http://www.newsweek.com/id/135380/page/2.

[2] Obama's green capitalism, based on green energy policies, is in part a response to the problem of global climate change but also, I would argue, also an ecological understanding of the global financial crisis and the undesirable network effects of financialization of the global economy. Obama's policies offer the possibility for a new wave of growth based on clean-green technologies for a low-carbon economy and forms of economic sustainability based on renewal resources.

[3] See the website on green economics at http://www.greeneconomics.net/ and the site on ecological economics at http://www.greeneconomics.net/.

[4] See http://en.wikipedia.org/wiki/Ecological_economics.

[5] This section draws on Peters and Hung (2009) and entries by Michael A. Peters in *New learning: A charter for change in education* at http://education.illinois.edu/newlearning/.

[6] See http://www.hawking.org.uk/lectures/bot.html.

REFERENCES

Alcott, B. (2005). Jevon's paradox, *Ecological Economics*, *54*, 9-21.

Brenan, A. & Lo, Y.-S. (2008). Environmental ethics, *Stanford Encyclopaedia of Philosophy*, at http://plato.stanford.edu/entries/ethics-environmental/.

Brundtland, G. (Ed.) (1987). *Our common future: World Commission on Environment and Development*. New York: Oxford University Press.

Friedman, Thomas (2008). Hot, flat and crowded: Why we need a green revolution – and how it can renew America. New York: Farrar, Straus and Giroux.

Gonzalez-Gaudiano, E.J. & Peters, M.A. (Eds.) (2008). *Environmental education today: Identity, politics and citizenship*. Rotterdam: Sense Publishers.

Greenwood, Dan (2007). The halfway house: Democracy, complexity, and the limits to markets in green political economy, *Environmental Politics*, *16*(1), 73-91.

Hall, Charles (2004). The myth of sustainable development: Personal reflections on energy, its relation to neoclassical economics, and Stanley Jevon, *Journal of Energy Resources Technology*, *26*, 85-89.

Hermann, E. Daly & Farley, Joshua (2004). *Ecological economics: Principles and applications*. New York: Island Press.

Ikerd, J. (2005). *Sustainable capitalism*. West Hartford: Kumarian Press.

Kapitzke, C. & Peters, Michael A. (Eds.) (2006). *Global knowledge cultures*. Rotterdam: Sense Publishers.

Mayumi, K., Giampietro, M., & Alcott, B. (2008). *Jevon's paradox and the myth of resource efficiency improvements*. London: Earthscan Publications.

Mason, Mark (Ed.) (2008). Complexity theory and the philosophy of education. *Educational Philosophy and Theory* (Special Issue), *40*(1), 4-18.

Merchant, C. (1990). *The death of nature: Women, ecology, and the scientific revolution*. New York: HarperOne.

O'Connor, James (1993). Is sustainable capitalism possible? In P. Allen (Ed.), *Food for the Future* (pp. 125-138). New York: Wiley.

Peters, Michael A. (2007). *Knowledge economy, development and the future of higher education*. Rotterdam: Sense Publishers.

Peters, Michael A. (2008). Complexity and knowledge systems. In M. Mason (Ed.), *Complexity Theory and the Philosophy of Education, Educational Philosophy and Theory*, Special Issue, *40*(1), 1-3.

Peters, Michael A. & Araya, D. (2009). Network logic: An ecological approach to knowledge and learning. In M. McKenzie, H. Bai, B. Jickling, & and P. Hart (Eds), *Fields of green: Re-imagining education*. New Jersey: Hampton Press.

Peters, Michael A. & Besley, Tina (A.C.) (2006). *Building knowledge cultures: Education and development in the age of knowledge capitalism*. Lanham/Oxford: Boulder, NY/Rowman & Littlefield.

Peters, Michael A. & Britez, Rodrigo (2008). *Open education and education for openness*. Rotterdam: Sense.

Peters, Michael A. & Hung, Ruyu (2009). Solar ethics: A new paradigm for environmental ethics? In E.J. Gonzalez-Gaudiano & M.A. Peters (Eds.), *Environmental education today: Identity, politics and citizenship*. Rotterdam: Sense Publishers.

Peters, Michael A. & Roberts, P. (2009). *The Virtues of Openness*. Boulder: Paradigm Publishers.

Peters, Michael A., Marginson, Simon, & Murphy, Peter (2009). *Creativity and the global knowledge economy*. New York: Peter Lang.

Prigogine, I. (1997). *The end of certainty*. The Free Press: New York.

Putnam, R. (2000). *Bowling alone: The collapse and revival of American community*. New York: Simon and Schuster.

Rifkin, Jeremy (2003). *The hydrogen economy*. New York: Tarcher.

Ross, M. (2008). Expansion of the universe – Standard Big Bang model, at http://arxiv.org/PS_cache/arxiv/pdf/0802/0802.2005v1.pdf.

Stiglitz, J. (1999a). Knowledge for development: Economic science, economic policy, and economic advice. In *Proceedings from the Annual Bank Conference on Development Economics 1998* (pp. 9-58). Washington D.C.: World Bank, Keynote Address.

Stiglitz, Joseph E. (July 1999b). Knowledge as a global public good, *Global Public Goods*, 308-326.

White, L. (1967). The historical roots of our ecological crisis. *Science, 55*, 1203-1207.

Willers, B. (1994). Sustainable development: A new world deception, *Conservation Biology, 8*(4), 1146-1148.

York, R., Clark, B., & Foster, Bellamy J. (May 2009). Capitalism in wonderland: Why mainstream economist can't deal with the crisis, *Monthly Review*. Retrieved September 8, 2009, from https://www.monthlyreview.org/090501-york-clark-foster.php.

CHAPTER 8

OBAMA'S 'POSTMODERNISM', HUMANISM
AND HISTORY *

April is the cruellest month, breeding
Lilacs out of the dead land, mixing
Memory and desire, stirring
Dull roots with spring rain.
Winter kept us warm, covering
Earth in forgetful snow, feeding
A little life with dried tubers.

T.S. Eliot's (1922) *The waste land*

Just when we all thought that debates about postmodernism had been consigned to the history of theory – to the 1980s culture wars – like a many-headed serpent it has raised its head once more. In spite of the fact that Jean-François Lyotard (1984) had carefully explained that postmodernism is not modernism at its end but in its nascent and (constant) state, many commentators throughout the 1980s and after insisted on treating postmodernism in terms of a strict chronology. Remember? 'A work can become modern only if it is first postmodern, for postmodernism is not modernism at its end but in its nascent state, that is, at the moment it attempts to present the unpresentable, and this state is constant' (Lyotard, 1984, p. 79). The postmodern for Lyotard, then, is a repetition of the modern as the 'new', and this means the ever-new demand for another repetition. Wilful misunderstanding, deliberate misreading has accompanied the postmodern debates from the outset. I am thinking in particular of Habermas' (1981) wildly polemical attack on French thinkers such as Foucault, Lyotard and Derrida, a position he was to reverse a couple of decades later (Peters, 1994).

I have chosen to start with a stanza from T.S. Eliot's *The waste land* because it symbolizes so clearly the cultural stakes associated with modernism and anti-modernism, a dialectic we must comes to terms with if we are to understand its counterparts, postmodernism and antipostmodernism. The poem itself is an exploration of the soul's struggle for regeneration and Eliot's viewpoint, developed in the essay *Tradition and the individual talent* (Eliot, 1920) relating to the theory of the

* I would like to thank Simon Marginson, Bill Cope, and Fazal Rizvi for constructive comments on an earlier version of this chapter.

unity of the soul, suggests that the poet has a *medium* rather than a personality to express, a medium within which to record impressions and experiences that combine as he says 'in peculiar and unexpected ways'. *The waste land* is fragmentary poem, a series of monologues that reference different voices and cultural allusions in musical phrases that overlap one another where the waste land itself is thrown into relief against symbols of regeneration and rebirth.

The term 'postmodernism' has recently been used to describe President Barack Obama and not by just one commentator. Jonah Goldberg in a recent *USA Today* column,[1] the author of *Liberal fascism*, advanced the notion that Obama is a postmodernist. Goldberg provides the following characterization

> An explosive fad in the 1980s, postmodernism was and is an enormous intellectual hustle in which left-wing intellectuals take crowbars and pick axes to anything having to do with the civilizational Mount Rushmore of Dead White European Males.

'PoMos' hold that there is no such thing as capital-T 'Truth'. There are only lower-case 'truths'. Our traditional understandings of right and wrong, true and false, are really just ways for those Pernicious Pale Patriarchs to keep the Coalition of the Oppressed in their place. In the PoMo's telling, reality is 'socially constructed'. And so the PoMos seek to tear down everything that 'privileges' the powerful over the powerless and to replace it with new truths more to their liking.

Hence the deep dishonesty of postmodernism. It claims to liberate society from fixed meanings and rigid categories, but it is invariably used to impose new ones, usually in the form of political correctness. We've all seen how adept the PC brigades are celebrating free speech, when it's for speech they like.

He goes on to write:

> Asked to define sin, Barack Obama replied that sin is 'being out of alignment with my values'. Statements such as this have caused many people to wonder whether Obama has a God complex or is hopelessly arrogant. For the record, sin isn't being out of alignment with your own values (if it were, Hannibal Lecter wouldn't be a sinner because his values hold that it's OK to eat people) nor is it being out of alignment with Obama's' unless he really is our Savior ...

Obama gives every indication of having evolved from this intellectual soup. As a student and, later, a law school instructor, Obama was sympathetic to Critical Race Theory, a wholly owned franchise of postmodernism. At Harvard, Obama revered Derrick Bell, a controversial Black law professor who preferred personally defined literary truths over old-fashioned literal truth. 'Words are power', Bell and Co. argued, 'and your so-called facts are merely myths of the White power structure'.

Goldberg is not the only source for this monstrous characterization.[2] Webster Griffin Tarpley, Bruce Marshall and Jonathon Mowat (2008) have written a book entitled *Obama: The postmodern coup* that purportedly exposes Obama from the Left arguing that Obama is in reality 'a right-winger, an elitist, a creature of Wall Street, and a deeply troubled personality, running far to the right of his main opponent' (then Senator and now Secretary Clinton).[3]

But this book is not the one that caught my eye: Barack Obama is 'postmodern' or at least so thinks Cardinal James Francis Stafford, a high-ranking Papal official. This is the attribution that in my view requires serious attention although I will not attempt to defend Obama against these spurious charges. Rather I will try to make clear the ideological nature of Catholic unvarnished humanism and the role it plays in the spiritual history and scientific progress of mankind.

In an address to the Catholic University of America on November 13, 2008 Cardinal Stafford covered a wide-ranging set of topics which he describes in his paper as:

> the narrow, calculative, mathematical mind and its manipulation of the *humanum* and, more specifically, of human sexuality since 1968; the response of the Church's magisterium in the encyclical letter of Pope Paul VI, *Humanae Vitae* and teachings of later Popes; other Catholic philosophical and theological responses to what John Rawls calls the 'embedding module', namely the increasingly disenchanted world in which we work and pray.

In this context Cardinal Stafford details the 'moral chaos' that ensued since Woodstock in 1968 to the exhausting of America in 2008 singling out for comment and criticism the 1973 U.S. Supreme Courts' pro-abortion decision that he asserts 'was imposed upon the nation'. In this line of thinking he suggests 'The President-elect is a skillful rhetorician. Civic life has been invaded with an anti-humanism so toxic that it is proving mortal to the body politic'. The anti-humanism is constituted through 'complex strategies of power' that have invaded the nation and caused freedom to be sacrificed to power. In particular, Cardinal Stafford expresses his anxiety about the intervening 40 years and the use of 'widespread contraceptive practice' that he describes in Biblical terms and consequences which suffers from a new economic mentality applied to human beings and their essences (appealing to Heidegger). In the course of this narrative Cardinal Stafford write of the real object of his criticism:

> In the United States President-elect Barack Obama and the Vice-President-elect Joseph Biden, a Catholic, campaigned on a severe anti-life platform. Robert P. George, McCormick Professor of Jurisprudence and Director of the James Madison Program in American Ideals and Institutions at Princeton University and a member of the President's Council on Bioethics, analyzed America's descent since 1968-1973 into deathworks by summarizing Obama's vision. George's analysis appeared in the journal, *Public Discourse*. '[Obama] has co-sponsored a bill ... that would authorize the large-scale industrial production of human embryos for use in biomedical research in which they would be killed. In fact, the bill Obama co-sponsored would effectively require the killing of human beings in the embryonic stage that were produced by cloning'.

Stafford is responding to and criticizing Obama's pre-election stated intention to reverse the 2001 decision by President Bush to limit stem cell research banning the use of human embryonic stem cells. Obama lifted restrictions on federal funding for medical research using human embryonic stem cells on March 9, 2009 which he pictured as part of a broader effort to limit political interference in science suggesting that Bush's decision was wrong and based on a false choice between sound science and moral values.[4] Obama argues that the two are not inconsistent especially as scientific work is used to care for others and ease human suffering. Obama said that his order is meant to restore 'scientific integrity to government decision-making' and indicated it was the beginning of a process of ensuring his administration bases its decision on sound science; appoints scientific advisers based on their credentials, not their politics; and promotes free and open inquiry.

Cardinal Stafford's argument is about a form of Catholic humanism that has a history of Church ideological intervention in science going back at least to Galileo. As most people know Galileo, the father of observational astronomy and modern science, defended his heliocentric Copenican theory of the universe against charges of heresy levelled at him by prominent members of the Church including Cardinal Bellarmine. He then stood trial against these charges in Rome in 1633 and was found guilty on the basis that his theory was contrary to Holy Scripture and he was forced to recant. This was a major blow to the progress and acceptance of his work and of science at that time. It was only in 1758 that the general prohibition of his works was lifted and on 31 October 1992, John Paul II officially conceded that the Earth was not stationary. In March 2008 the Vatican vindicated Galileo by erecting a statue of him inside the Vatican.

Stafford appeals to Heidegger's essentialism and his attacks on technology to criticize the 'scientific and technological hegemony' that characterizes Obama's outlook and leads to the 'deathworks' of postmodern society. This appeal is curious given Heidegger's (1947) famous 'Letter on humanism' where responding to the question '*Comment redonner un sense au mot "Humanisme"?*' he embarks on an analysis of the history, meaning and the truth of Being indicating that the first humanism was Roman, as an exaltation of Greek ideals which transmutes during the Italian Renaissance of the 14 and 15 centuries. And then he remarks:

> But if one understands by humanism in general man's effort to become free for his humanness and to find in it his dignity, then the meaning of humanism is different depending upon one's conception of 'freedom' and of the 'nature' of man.

And he amplifies this statement stating:

> Every humanism is either grounded in metaphysics or makes itself the ground of some metaphysics. Every determination of the essence of man that already presupposes a reading of be-ing, without [raising] the question of the truth of *be*[-ing] – be it intentionally or unintentionally – is metaphysical.[5]

Stafford returns to the texts of John Paul II and Benedict XVI to christen the sanctity of the relationship between spouses in a marriage relationship. His object of critique is of course same-sex marriage. The present crisis he concludes is ontological/epistemological and linguistic and the response he suggests is to root language, especially that of the human body, in ontology:

A solidly unabashed metaphysics of being, founded on the real distinction between essence and existence, is essential for any recovery of truth and its objective structure. Postmodernists have rejected the tradition of western metaphysics, the concept of being since Socrates, and the real distinction between essence and existence.

He encourages Catholic scholars to explore 'the nuptial language founded upon the biblical text and upon the Catholic tradition and enriched by the teaching of John Paul II' and 'the relationship between the nuptial meaning of the human body and the Eucharist, as the triform Body of Christ'. The Cardinal risks prediction but also implicitly issues a call to arms: 'if Obama, Biden and the new Congress are determined to implement the anti-life agenda which they spelled out before the election, I foresee the next several years as being among the most divisive in our nation's history'. Cardinal Stafford correctly identifies the importance of *The Freedom of Choice Act* and the centrality of *Roe* to Obama's constitutional vision. Obama is 'postmodern' because he is 'pro-choice' and not 'pro-life'; and also because he supports gay rights and same-sex marriage on the same principle of individual choice. What is postmodern about this position? Obama is perceived as embracing an alleged moral relativism – this is the traditional accusation accompanying such claims.[6]

The Cardinal does not mention the historic Catholic antimodernism or the consistently reactionary position of the Catholic Church on many issues of value.[7] In 1907, Pius X issued the encyclicals *Lamentabili* and *Pascendi dominici gregis* to combat what he called 'Modernism', a faith-corrupting force. In 1910, Pius X's witch-hunt climaxed with *Sacrorum Antistitum*,[8] an oath against Modernist philosophy to be taken by all Catholic clergy and theologians that began:

As solidly unabashed metaphysics of being.
And first of all, I profess that God, the origin and end of all things, can be known with certainty by the natural light of reason from the created world (see Rom. 1:90), that is, from the visible works of creation, as a cause from its effects, and that, therefore, his existence can also be demonstrated. Secondly, I accept and acknowledge the external proofs of revelation, that is, divine acts and especially miracles and prophecies as the surest signs of the divine origin of the Christian religion and I hold that these same proofs are well adapted to the understanding of all eras and all men, even of this time.

The third article confirms the Church as the guardian and teacher of the revealed word, was personally instituted by the real and historical Christ and Peter's apostolic hierarchy where the fourth article confirms the doctrine of faith and rejects 'the heretical misrepresentation that dogmas evolve and change from one meaning to another different from the one which the Church held previously'. (Of course, the Church based on a literalness would reject hermeneutics of change and context.) Fifth, the encyclical held that faith is not psychological but is genuine assent of intellect and went on to reject 'the error of those who say that the faith held by the Church can contradict history, and that Catholic dogmas, in the sense in which they are now understood, are irreconcilable with a more realistic view of the origins of the Christian religion'. It reject all forms of textualism and methods of judging and interpreting Sacred Scripture that depart from the tradition of the Church as well as interpretation based on solely by scientific principles that excludes sacred authority, and encourages 'the same liberty of judgment that is common in the investigation of all ordinary historical documents'.

Finally, I declare that I am completely opposed to the error of the modernists who hold that there is nothing divine in sacred tradition; or what is far worse, say that there is, but in a pantheistic sense, with the result that there would remain nothing but this plain simple fact-one to be put on a par with the ordinary facts of history-the fact, namely, that a group of men by their own labor, skill, and talent have continued through subsequent ages a school begun by Christ and his apostles.

Catholic antimodernism is reactionary, dogmatic and fundamentalist as is Catholic and Marxist antipostmoderism, and in much the same ways. The Cardinal conveniently appeals to Heidegger's essentialism, also based on Catholic antimodernism as well as ideas of *völkisch* movement,[9] and Nietzsche's *Will to power*. There is also a legitimate antimodernist radical ecology and the critique of industrialism and modernity's nihilistic 'enframing' of everything as raw material ('standing reserve'). If the essence of 'modernism' is progress based on the belief that technological development means economic development, the core assumption of antimodernism draws our attention to the fact that 'progress' has a dark side – that technologically-driven industrialism has destroyed large areas of nature, dislocated communities, endangered culture and spirituality. Some forms of postmodernism draw on this strain of antimodernism to emphasize romantic literary convention and the revolt against calculative or instrumental reason in both Marxist and Weberian senses. Some also drew on the critiques of industrial labour – the artisanal critiques of labor made by John Ruskin, William Morris, and the Arts and Craft Movement – as well as Marx's theory of alienation. Perhaps, what this form of antimodernist postmodernism revealed was the centrality of the question of modernity itself. As Foucault (1986) writes:

the question of modernity has been posed in classical culture according to an axis with two poles, antiquity and modernity; it had been formulated either in terms of an authority to be accepted or rejected ... or else in the form ... of a comparative evaluation: are the Ancients superior to the Moderns? are we living in a period of decadence? and so forth. There now appears a new way of posing the question of modernity, no longer within a longitudinal relationship to the Ancients, but rather in what one might call a 'sagital' relation to one's own present-ness. Discourse has to take account of its own present-ness, in order to find its own place, to pronounce its meaning, and to specify the mode of action which it is capable of exercising within this present. What is my present? What is the meaning of this present? Such is, it seems to me, the substance of this new interrogation on modernity. (p. 90)

Arthur C. Danto (2004) indicates that:

For Hegel, the world in its historical dimension is the dialectical revelation of consciousness to itself. In his curious idiom, the end of history comes when

Spirit achieves awareness of its identity as Spirit, not, that is to say, alienated from itself by ignorance of its proper nature, but united to itself through itself: by recognizing that it is in this one instance of the same substance as it subject, since consciousness of consciousness is consciousness. (pp. 15-16)

And yet for Derrida and others there has never been a self-transparent, self-present subject: 'The Subject is a fable'. Derrida's relation to Hegel (and Hegelian modernity) is one based on the attempt to undermine the very heart of the idealist project. His attack on 'logocentrism' is simultaneously an attack on the history of philosophy (Hegel's philosophical history) as a history of consciousness or Spirit achieving awareness of its own identity. There is no standpoint outside of history or of conceiving past times as stages on the way to the present. History is not linear. Each age tries to its own present as 'new'. In this respect, Nietzsche would agree with Charles Baudelaire, who describes modernity as 'the transient, the fleeting, the contingent' that is repeated in all ages. Modernist thinkers like Kant, Hegel and Marx held that history is cumulative and progressive and man is progressing inevitably toward a 'perfect constitution', a maximally free civil society.

But Foucault and Derrida see history, like Nietzsche saw God, as 'ending' in the sense of 'dying', and think the progressive character of history is lost article of faith belonging to a bygone age. They criticize the anthropocentrism of Enlightenment humanism and science that postulates Man as pinnacle and controller of Nature. There is no predictable overall pattern in history and modern society is not necessary better or enlightened in comparison to the pre-modern or the primitive societies. Foucault attacks Marxism because it believes that it has discovered the secret of history and historical development. Yet Foucault reminds us there is no rational course to history and certainly not one we can state in advance nor is there any over-arching telos to history. Our past is always an invention of our present. History, knowledge and the human subject are fundamentally rooted in contingency, discontinuity, iniquitous origins and the struggle for power. Hegel and Marx are the 'philosophes' who believed in the progressive journey of history but now the Enlightenment philosophy of 'world history' as a systematic and overarching project has failed and been revealed as the equivalent of an Orientalism in literature or the arts. Most of us now have come to believe with cosmological physicists and biologists in the irreducible contingency and indeterminacy of all events, including human events, that cannot be encapsulated in a conception of 'world history' (or at least not yet, although the speed and extent of globalization might change that too).

NOTES

[1] See http://blogs.usatoday.com/oped/2008/08/obama-the-postm.html.

[2] See Jane Kim's response, indicating that apparently being postmodern is better than being post-racial and writing: If that's Goldberg's contention – that the Obama condition, perhaps most reflected in the press's oft-surprising ineptness, is an un-pinnable one – then, hey, he should come on board (and read Megan Garber's take on that topic, via David Brooks, while he's at it), and congratulate Obama's *campaign* for being postmodern in its narrative-building' at

http://www.cjr.org/campaign_desk/obamas_postmodern_condition.php. In this respect see the post on the Minnesota Family Council site at http://mnfamilycouncil.blogspot.com/2008/08/obama-postmodernism-and-definition-of.html. See also 'Obama's Reactionary Postmodernism' at http://herdgadfly.blogspot.com/2008/08/obamas-reactionary-postmodernism.html.

[3] This book argues (product description) 'Barack Obama is a deeply troubled personality, the mega-lomaniac front man for a postmodern coup by the intelligence agencies, using fake polls, mobs of swarming adolescents, super-rich contributors, and orchestrated media hysteria to short-circuit normal politics and seize power. Obama comes from the orbit of the Ford Foundation, and has never won public office in a contested election. His guru and controller is Zbigniew Brzezinski, the deranged revanchist and Russia-hater who dominated the catastrophic Carter presidency 30 years ago. All indications are that Brzezinski recruited Obama at Columbia University a quarter century ago. Trilateral Commission co-founder Brzezinski wants a global showdown with Russia and China far more dangerous for the United States than the Bush-Cheney Iraq adventure'. Need I say more?

[4] See the video of Obama's decision on YouTube at http://www.youtube.com/watch?v= 2Gs39k0IxZ0. The executive order can be viewed at http://www.cryptome.com/0001/eo13505.htm. For a brief discussion of the politics of stem cell research see http://www.pbs.org/wgbh/nova/sciencenow/dispatches/050413.html.

[5] I am using the translation provided by Miles Groth at http://www.wagner.edu/departments/psychology/filestore2/download/101/MartinHeideggerLETTER_ON_HUMANISM.pdf.

[6] See my 'Renewing the American dream: Obama's political philosophy' (Peters, 2009).

[7] See my discussion of John Paul II encyclical *Orthos Logos, Recta Ratio* that discusses postmodernism.

[8] For the full oath see http://www.fisheaters.com/sacrorum.html.

[9] A German interpretation of the populist movement, with a romantic focus on folklore and the 'organic' defining a dream for a self-sufficient life lived with a mystical relation to the land.

REFERENCES

Bennett, David (2009). *Perspectives on postmodernism: Sampling Australian composers*. Australian Music Centre.

Danto, Arthur C. (2004). *The philosophical disenfranchisement of art*. New York: Columbia University Press.

Eliot (1920). Tradition and the individual talent. In *The sacred wood: Essays on poetry and criticism* at http://www.bartleby.com/200/sw4.html.

Foucault, M. (February 1986). Kant on enlightenment and revolution (trans. Colin Gordon), *Economy and Society*, *15*(1), 88-96.

Habermas, Jurgen (Winter, 1981). Modernity vs postmodernity, *New German Critique*, Special Issue on Modernism, *22*, 3-14.

Henderson, Margaret (1998). Some origins of species: Postmodern theories in Australia, *Journal of Australian Studies*, *57*, 50-60.

Kitching, Gavin (August 2008). Paralysed by postmodernism, *Australian Literary Review of The Australian*, *3*(7).

Lyotard, Jean-François (1984). *The postmodern condition: A report on knowledge*. Manchester: Manchester University Press.

Peters, Michael A. (September 1994). Habermas, poststructuralism and the question of postmodernity: The defiant periphery, *Social Analysis*, *36*, 1-18.

Peters, Michael A. (2000). *Orthos logos, recta ratio*: Pope John Paul II, nihilism and postmodern philosophy, *Journal for Christian Theological Research*, *5*, http://home.apu.edu/~CTRF/jctr.html.

Peters, Michael A. (2001). *Poststructuralism, Marxism and neoliberalism: Between theory and politics*. Rowman & Littlefield.

Peters, Michael A. (2009). Renewing the American dream: Obama's political philosophy, *Policy Futures in Education*, *7*(1), 125-128.

Peters, Michael A. & Marshall, J.D. (1999). *Wittgenstein: Philosophy, postmodernism, pedagogy*. Westport, CT & London: Bergin & Garvey.

Peters, Micahel A., Burbules, N., & Smeyers, P. (2008). *Saying and doing: Wittgenstein as a pedagogical philosopher*. Boulder, CO: Paradigm Press.

Solas, John (2001). The poverty of postmodern human services, *Australian Social Work*, 55(2), 128-135.

Tarpley, Webster Griffin, Marshall, Bruce, & Mowat, Jonathon (2008). *Obama: The postmodern coup*. Progressive Press.

Windschuttle, Keith (2006). The return of postmodernism in Aboriginal history, *Quadrant* at http://www.sydneyline.com/Return%20of%20Postmodernism.htm.

CHAPTER 9

'WINNING THE FUTURE'

The United States of America faces a critical series of challenges that will determine its role in world affairs. Some, like Fareed Zakaria (2009), argue that we are living in a post-American world. Clearly the rise of China, India, Brazil and the growth of African economies spurred by China's acquisition and securing of raw materials and long term trade options now have become among the fastest growing in the world. The logic of globalization is changing and the disastrous financial crisis and its spread effects have hastened the decline of the U.S. and its relative position as global investor and peace-keeper.

There have been 47 recessions in the U.S. since 1790, 13 since the Great Depression. The most recent economic downturn contributed to a global financial crisis that led to the failure or collapse of many of the United States' largest financial institutions including Bears Stern, Fannie Mae, Freddie Mac, Lehmann Brothers and the giant insurance company AIG (American International Group). The Bush government responded with an unprecedented $700 billion bank bailout (The Emergency Economic Stabilization Act of 2008) proposed by Henry Paulson named TARP (Troubled Assets Relief Program) and used to purchase failing bank assets. This was an amazing turnaround for a government of the free market that was intended to prevent further erosion of confidence in the U.S. credit markets that could have led to a massive global depression. In a radical move government intervention was suddenly back in favor. Paulson summarized the rationale for the bailout before the U.S. Senate by arguing that it would stabilize markets and improve liquidity and provide time for a comprehensive review of the regulatory framework. The plan was criticized by academic economists as basically unfair, ambiguous and with uncertain long-term effects.

On assuming office President Obama instituted a $787 billion fiscal stimulus package (The American Recovery and Reinvestment Act of 2009). The Act includes federal tax cuts ($288 billion), expansion of unemployment benefits ($82.5 billion) and other social welfare provisions and domestic spending in education ($90.0 billion), health care ($147.7 billion), and infrastructure ($80.9 billion), including the energy sector ($61.3 billion), housing ($12.7 billion), scientific research ($8.9 billion) and other projects ($18.1 billion). Economists are almost equally divided on the stimulus package with Keynesian and neo-Keynesians like Paul Krugman and Joseph Stiglitz favoring the large stimulus package and Austrian and Chicago School economists criticizing the government's plan.

Global free market economics Chicago school style has spelt the end of the monetarist consensus about the self-healing capacity of the market and prominent economists suggested that Keynes is back in fashion. The costs have been enormous and almost beyond precise calculation. The International Monetary Fund (IMF) in its Global Financial Stability Report indicated that U.S. institutions were about half way through their loss cycle and needed write-downs, while their European counterparts are still lagging. Banks will bear about two-thirds of the write-downs, which are coming on $58 trillion of debt originating in the United States, Europe and Japan. Altman (2009:5) makes the following estimates:

> Total home equity in the United States, which was valued at $13 trillion at its peak in 2006, had dropped to $8.8 trillion by mid-2008 and was still falling in late 2008. Total retirement assets, Americans' second-largest household asset, dropped by 22 percent, from $10.3 trillion in 2006 to $8 trillion in mid-2008. During the same period, savings and investment assets (apart from retirement savings) lost $1.2 trillion and pension assets lost $1.3 trillion. Taken together, these losses total a staggering $8.3 trillion.

In the period since 2007 over 140 U.S. banks have failed. The aftermath of the banking crisis has been associated with massive increases in unemployment and declines in output. Unemployment has been running over 10% during much of 2008-2010.

New Zealand and Australia has been cushioned against the worst effects of recession in part because of its proximity to Asia: Australia because of its mineral wealth and the so-called parallel economy – mining is doing very well – and the Australian banks were not invested heavily in the U.S. housing market; New Zealand largely because of the strength of its diary industry.

Reinhart and Rogoff (2008) suggest that 'the present U.S. financial crisis is severe by any metric.' Many have pointed to the systemic nature of the crisis. Gokay (2009) suggests an analysis in terms of 'the explosive growth of the financial system during the last three decades relative to manufacturing and the economy as a whole' with the huge growth of finance capitalism and 'the proliferation of speculative and destabilising financial institutional arrangements and instruments of wealth accumulation.' This has meant 'the rise of new centres and the loss of relative weight of the U.S. as a global hegemonic power' with increasing resource depletion and ecological crisis. He goes on to argue:

> The current financial crisis (and economic downturn) has not come out of blue. It is the outcome of deep-seated contradictions within the structure of global economic system. It is not a 'failure' of the system, but it is central to the mode of functioning of the system itself. It is not the result of some 'mistakes' or 'deviations,' but rather it is inherent to the logic of the system.

He asks 'Is this the end of capitalism?' to which he responds 'There is nothing to suggest that the present crisis is paving the way for the collapse of the capitalist system. It signifies the opening of a new epoch in history, in which some of the old structures give way and new forms may develop to radically affect the global structures of power and hegemony.'

It is against this grim background that President Obama gave his 2011 State of the Union address. While Obama policies prevented a decline into a deepening depression they have not yet produced the expected growth or productivity gains and much of his address was given over to the economy and the creation of jobs. The speech was called 'winning the future' and while not a typical inspiring speech from the heart, it was carefully crafted to reach all political constituencies and to provide some basis for governing after the Republicans took Congress in the mid term elections.[1]

The speech gave a ritual nod to the new speaker of the House and remembered the shooting at Tucson. Obama appealed to the higher union, 'the American family' and American democracy that sets it apart from other countries. He also made reference to a 'new era of cooperation' before turning his attention to the economy itemizing his policies and the progress that has been made while at the same time indicating that the world had fundamentally changed.

The rules have changed. In a single generation, revolutions in technology have transformed the way we live, work and do business. Steel mills that once needed 1,000 workers can now do the same work with 100. Today, just about any company can set up shop, hire workers, and sell their products wherever there's an Internet connection.

Meanwhile, nations like China and India realized that with some changes of their own, they could compete in this new world. And so they started educating their children earlier and longer, with greater emphasis on math and science. They're investing in research and new technologies. Just recently, China became the home to the world's largest private solar research facility, and the world's fastest computer.

It is against this rhetoric that Obama embarks on the major theme of the speech 'winning the future'. As he says 'The future is ours to win' and he introduces the theme in this way:

Sustaining the American Dream has never been about standing pat. It has required each generation to sacrifice, and struggle, and meet the demands of a new age.

And now it's our turn. We know what it takes to compete for the jobs and industries of our time. We need to out-innovate, out-educate, and out-build the rest of the world. (Applause.) We have to make America the best place on Earth to do business. We need to take responsibility for our deficit and reform our government. That's how our people will prosper. That's how we'll win the future. (Applause.) And tonight, I'd like to talk about how we get there.

Obama's answer? American innovation. Creativity and imagination. The free enterprise system that drives innovation. Investment in science and technology ('this is our sputnik moment'). And more specifically, investment in renewable and clean energy. Perhaps, most importantly (and predictably) education.

Maintaining our leadership in research and technology is crucial to America's success. But if we want to win the future – if we want innovation to produce jobs in America and not overseas – then we also have to win the race to educate our kids.

The philosophy of globalization and winning the future is education and the philosophy of education is 'Race to the Top.' Let me quote extensively from the speech on centrality of education to Obama's vision for America in winning the future:

> Think about it. Over the next 10 years, nearly half of all new jobs will require education that goes beyond a high school education. And yet, as many as a quarter of our students aren't even finishing high school. The quality of our math and science education lags behind many other nations. America has fallen to ninth in the proportion of young people with a college degree. And so the question is whether all of us – as citizens, and as parents – are willing to do what's necessary to give every child a chance to succeed.
>
> That responsibility begins not in our classrooms, but in our homes and communities. It's family that first instills the love of learning in a child. Only parents can make sure the TV is turned off and homework gets done. We need to teach our kids that it's not just the winner of the Super Bowl who deserves to be celebrated, but the winner of the science fair. (Applause.) We need to teach them that success is not a function of fame or PR, but of hard work and discipline.
>
> Our schools share this responsibility. When a child walks into a classroom, it should be a place of high expectations and high performance. But too many schools don't meet this test. That's why instead of just pouring money into a system that's not working, we launched a competition called Race to the Top. To all 50 states, we said, "If you show us the most innovative plans to improve teacher quality and student achievement, we'll show you the money."
>
> Race to the Top is the most meaningful reform of our public schools in a generation. For less than 1% of what we spend on education each year, it has led over 40 states to raise their standards for teaching and learning. And these standards were developed, by the way, not by Washington, but by Republican and Democratic governors throughout the country. And Race to the Top should be the approach we follow this year as we replace No Child Left Behind with a law that's more flexible and focused on what's best for our kids. (Applause.)

What kind of vision is this? It seems remarkably mechanistic, reductionistic, and smack of a kind of neoliberalism that focuses on 'what works' on holding teachers responsible for America's success, on the hiring and firing of teachers, on penalizing bad teachers, on testing and regulation, on STEM, on investment in science, math and technology education. There is the genuflection to teachers in South Korea as 'nation builders' and Obama remarks: 'If you want to make a difference in the life of our nation; if you want to make a difference in the life of a child – become a teacher. Your country needs you.'

Obama also mentions higher education and the plight of the children of undocumented workers born in the U.S.

Innovation, education, rebuilding America (the third step) – that is, mending and improving the infrastructure, simplifying the tax code, reducing barriers to growth and investment, and debt management and reduction.

This is the 'new' prescription for America and restoring the America dream in an age of globalization dominated by fears and anxieties associated with the rise of China that has produced a kind of defensiveness (a defensive modernity) and tarnished the American dream that reached its peak in the late 1960s. Confidence has been badly shaken and no longer is there the supreme expectation of manifest destiny, of an American dream that remains unassailable. What interests me is the extent to which education is so central to the recovery of the dream and the way that heavy expectations will produce an even more competitive environment for education with a focus on delivering the expected benefits to win the future. It is a philosophy of globalization, education and modernity to be carefully investigated and evaluated.

We have truly passed the era that asks what kind of student and citizen we want to produce (the eco-subject of clean energy?), no longer character-building and nation-building in itself with an emphasis of equality for all but only in the service of winning the future. Welcome to the age of the entrepreneurial subject where education has truly passed into a world political economy of globalization.

NOTES

[1] For the official Whitehouse video of the address see http://www.whitehouse.gov/state-of-the-union-2011. Gracing the website is the stark figure that only one in four students in a U.S. graduate from high school. A transcript is available at http://www.whitehouse.gov/the-press-office/2011/01/25/remarks-president-state-union-address.

REFERENCES

Altman, R.C. (2009). The great crash, 2008: A geopolitical setback for the West. *Foreign Affairs*, http://tomweston.net/TheGreatCrash.pdf.

Gokay, B. (2009). The 2008 world economic crisis: Global shifts and faultlines, *Global Research*, http://www.globalresearch.ca/index.php?context=va&aid=12283.

Reinhart, C.A. & Rogoff, K.S. (2008). The aftermath of financial crises, http://www.economics.harvard.edu/faculty/rogoff/files/Aftermath.pdf.

Zarakaria, F. (2008). *The post-America world*. New York: W.W. Norton.

CHAPTER 10

THE EGYPTIAN REVOLUTION 2011

It is remarkable that in 2011 we had the opportunity to watch or view the current events involving mass protests and popular uprising against Mubarak's autocracy. As many commentators have pointed out it was like being a witness to history – a mass protest for democracy that contrasts strongly with Jihadism and the establishment of a caliphate. Yet somehow the world media focus also created an involvement of those in the West that have access to viewing through the major channels – BBC, CNN, Al Jazeera, perhaps more importantly, Facebook, Twitter and blogs – the bubble effect is also massively important to the Egyptian people who are protesting; they felt the eyes of the world upon them and they already knew the world significance and the stakes of their struggles for recognition and self-determination. The stakes were very high and could have led to massive bloodshed. Mubarak and his crony regime also knew this and it is in part the reason that early on he tried to cut all public communication and coverage of events: disabling the Internet; cutting off cell phone coverage; penalizing Al Jazeera; and instigating attacks on foreign journalists. Certainly, the new communication technologies were a significant part of the whole, but this new social media should not obscure other more fundamental political questions.

One of the most important questions is that mass popular protest already has a history in Egypt. We must remember that there were strong protests against the British as early as 1882 against the bombardment of Alexandria, and again in 1951 against British imperialism over the Suez Canal; against the Camp David Accords in 1978 that were viewed as a capitulation to Israel; against the Ayatollah Khomeini's Islamic revolution in 1979; against the peace pact with Israel in 1980; against Mubarak's fifth term in 2005; against Murabak's government in 2008. The history of modern Egypt is a history that begins with protests against British occupation when it became a protectorate in 1914. British troops did not leave until 1956. In effect Britain deposed the Khedive in 1914, replacing him with a family member who was made Sultan. There were huge popular protests against the imposition of martial law in Cairo in 1921 and a growing sense of nationalism and Egyptian identity. The Egyptian revolution of 1952 overthrew King Faruk and Nasser became leader not only of Egypt but of the Arab world promoting 'Arab socialism.'

Protest and mass uprisings are no stranger to modern Egypt, neither is the strong nationalist and democracy movements. The course of development under Mubarak following Sadat's populist era and war with Israel, began with his election after

Sadat's assassination in 1981. He was reconfirmed three times to 2005 although the popular referendums were questionable and while there was economic 'reform' – large-scale privatization in the 1990s – there has not been political reform during the autocratic rule of Mubarak. As many people have now pointed out the popular uprisings throughout Egypt are very problematic for the U.S. government as it exposes 'the hypocrisy of the rhetoric of being a shining light for democracy and free markets, and the reality of geopolitics' where the U.S. supports Murabak to the tune of $1.3 billion per year. In this context it is interesting to remind ourselves of Barack Obama's Cairo speech in 2009:

> I do have an unyielding belief that all people yearn for certain things: the ability to speak your mind and have a say in how you are governed; confidence in the rule of law and the equal administration of justice; government that is transparent and doesn't steal from the people; the freedom to live as you choose. Those are not just American ideas, they are human rights, and that is why we will support them everywhere.[1]

He goes on to say:

> government of the people and by the people sets a single standard for all who hold power: you must maintain your power through consent, not coercion; you must respect the rights of minorities, and participate with a spirit of tolerance and compromise; you must place the interests of your people and the legitimate workings of the political process above your party.

It is interesting that the U.S. government have been urged to pursue democracy in Egypt on many occasions previously and encouraged to live up to their rhetoric. Michele Dunne (2007) writing for *Policy outlook* in 'Time to pursue democracy in Egypt' argued:

> Egypt is in the early stages of a leadership succession that may swing the country toward greater openness and competition or toward consolidated authoritarianism. Whether or not the United States pursues democracy promotion will be a critical factor in the outcome and also will shape other Arabs' sense of U.S. seriousness.[2]

For a former State Department and White House Middle East specialist I find her conclusion interesting:

> Finally, the single most important thing the United States can do to promote political reform in Egypt is to pay consistent attention to the subject ... The United States can have a significant effect on opposition and civil society activists in Egypt despite widespread anger at many aspects of U.S. policy in the Middle East. Periodic public statements by the U.S. President and Secretary of State embolden reform advocates in Egypt by showing that outsiders are aware of what is going on. Such attention on the part of the United States will be particularly critical in the next several years, as Egyptians shape the contours of a new political era.

There has been no shortage of political theory in Egypt: most famously perhaps is the case of Sayyid Qutb who as an Islamic theologian was a leader of the Muslim Brotherhood in the 1950s and developed a political philosophy in his Islamic manifesto *Ma'alim fi-l-Tariq* (*Milestones*) where he advocated a political system derived from the principles of Sharia law in opposition to dictatorship. A number of 'democratic theorists' questioned his Islamic state and use of Jihad while reformist and conservative Muslims took exception to his understanding of Sharia, his ideas on social justice and particularly the banning of slavery. Sayyid Qutb's work became a basis for Al Qaeda: Osama Bin Laden knew Qutb's brother and Anwar al-Awlaki became acquainted with Qutb's works while imprisoned in the Yemen.

Of all the issues generated by the recent turn of events perhaps the most important is the question of legitimacy. Legitimacy has both descriptive and normative readings: Weber's three-fold descriptive analysis of legitimacy analyzes faith in a political order because of tradition, leadership charisma, and rational rule of law and by contrast, the normative conception of political legitimacy that:

> refers to some benchmark of acceptability or justification of political power or authority and – possibly – obligation. On the broadest view, legitimacy both explains why the use of political power by a particular body – a state, a government, or a democratic collective, for example – is permissible and why there is a pro tanto moral duty to obey its commands. On this view, if the conditions for legitimacy are not met, political institutions exercise power unjustifiably and the commands they might produce do then not entail any obligation to obey.[3]

Peters (2010) lays out the way in which legitimacy is seen to relate to political authority and the notion of political obligation before analyzing the sources of legitimacy in consent of the people (a 'voluntarist line of thought in Christian political philosophy'), in utilitarian theory in terms of beneficial consequences, and public reason and democratic approval, an important legacy of consent theory with its origins in Kant and Rousseau.

Yet 'In contemporary political philosophy, not everyone agrees that democracy is necessary for political legitimacy.' Here 'democratic instrumentalism' vies with 'pure procedurialist' conceptions. As Peters (2010) goes on to explain 'Political cosmopolitanism is the view that national communities are not the exclusive source of political legitimacy in the global realm' where the 'two main approaches to both international and global legitimacy: the state-centered approach and the people-centered approach.' The first argues that state not persons are the subjects of international morality; the second, suggests it is individuals – their rights and interests – that is the proper source of legitimacy.

Certainly, the question of legitimacy is a central issue for global democracy and the emergence of cosmopolitanism. I am still not convinced by arguments for cosmopolitanism and have written about it expressing my views elsewhere on cosmopolitanism, democracy promotion and development (Peters, 2010; see also Peters, 2004, 2008). Part of my concern is how easily these notions serve ideological purposes that divert from the interests of the people.

In Egypt's case, at this early stage, it seems that despite the paid oppositional pro-Murbarak anti-democratic forces and their attempt to create disorder through violence, this a historically a significant democratic movement of the people that has serious implications for the Arab world, for the Middle East, and for the relationship with Israel and the U.S. There is no going back and popular uprisings in Tunisia, Yemen, Jordan and other North African states indicate a wave of political reform and the prospect of new freedoms, if not the genuine sovereignty of the people.

NOTES

[1] For the video and full text of the speech see http://www.huffingtonpost.com/2009/06/04/obama-egypt-speech-video_n_211216.html.

[2] See the full text article at http://www.carnegieendowment.org/files/Dunne_Egypt_FINAL2.pdf.

[3] See F. Peter's (2010) entry at http://plato.stanford.edu/entries/legitimacy/.

REFERENCES

Peters, M.A. (Ed.) (2004). *Education, globalization and the state in the age of terrorism*. Lanham & Oxford: Paradigm Publishers.

Peters, M.A. (2008). The end of development as we know it: Fukuyama on democracy promotion and political development. In G. Richardson & A. Abdi (Eds.), *Decolonizing democratic education: Transcultural dialogues*. London: Routledge.

Peters, M.A. (2009). Welcome! Postscript on hospitality, cosmopolitanism, and the other. In Michael A. Peters (Ed.), *Derrida, deconstruction, and the politics of pedagogy*. Peter Lang.

Peters, M.A. (2010). Ideologies of educational mobilities and counter-practices of cosmopolitanism, *Educational Philosophy and Theory*, Editorial.

CHAPTER 11

OBAMA, EDUCATION AND THE END OF
THE AMERICAN DREAM

You have to describe your country in terms of what you passionately hope it will become, as well as in terms of what you know it to be now. You have to be loyal to a dream country rather than to the one you wake up to every morning. Unless such loyalty exists the ideal has no chance of becoming actual.

Richard Rorty (2008), *Achieving our country: Leftist thought in twentieth-century America*

I am the son of a black man from Kenya and a white woman from Kansas. I was raised with the help of a white grandfather who survived a Depression to serve in Patton's army during World War II and a white grandmother who worked on a bomber assembly line at Fort Leavenworth while he was overseas. I've gone to some of the best schools in America and lived in one of the world's poorest nations. I am married to a black American who carries within her the blood of slaves and slave owners – an inheritance we pass on to our two precious daughters. I have brothers, sisters, nieces, nephews, uncles and cousins, of every race and every hue, scattered across three continents, and for as long as I live, I will never forget that in no other country on earth is my story even possible.

Senator Barack Obama (2008), *A more perfect union*[1]

INTRODUCTION

Richard Rorty (1998) the American pragmatist philosopher begins his book *Achieving our country* with the comment 'National pride is to countries what self respect is to individuals: a necessary condition for self improvement' (p. 3). He provides a narrative re-crafting of the dream in pre-Vietnam America by reference to Walt Whitman and John Dewey. According to Rorty, Whitman and Dewey shaped the secular dream of America based on the notion of exceptionalism without reference to the divine – a society where all Americans would become mobilized as political agents in the cause of democracy. He argues that for Whitman and Dewey the conjunction of the concepts 'America' and 'democracy' is an essential part of a new description of what it is to be human. Rorty's success as a philosopher is

Figure 19.

related to his ability to tell a new story about America and the American Dream, to redescribe the past using a different vocabulary and to highlight how a new philosophical history can make us feel differently about who we are and who we might become. Rorty offers us a 'philosophy of hope', a philosophy based on the narrative of cultural invention, self-discovery and national self-creation.[2]

What Rorty's book also draws attention to is the power of narrative and the way in which the 'American Dream' is a specific narrative that comes into being at a particular time and place and then can be 'read back' on American history–on the puritan beginnings and those who wrote the Declaration and the Constitution. It is a narrative that can be 'read forward', projected onto the future, as a means of establishing a vision for a society and economy. This is the art of narrative retellings of the American Dream that in the hands of Rorty or Obama becomes a shining beacon to unify the people in recognizing what is best in America. The question is whether in a time of radical change and transition – when America is losing its world position as the only superpower, when millions of Americans are losing their homes and jobs as a result of the recession and financial crisis, when America enters into a massive budget-cutting and deficit financing mode – whether the America Dream can be reclaimed, refurbished, rearticulated and retold in era of decline.

Barack Obama is a skillful politician and great orator. He has consistently made reference to the American Dream in his campaigning for the presidency and after, often focusing on his own remarkable story as emblematic of the possible. He has also carefully used the intellectual resources of the American Dream to unify Americans and to provide the vision for the society he wants others to dream of. The question is in a time of decline how serviceable is this dream: can it be restored? Are its core ideals able to be refashioned?

Fareed Zakaria, like Obama, believes that it is possible to restore the America Dream and like millions of immigrants in developing countries remembers the attraction of America when growing up in India during the 1970s:

> The American dream for me, growing up in India in the 1970s, looked something like the opening credits of *Dallas*. The blockbuster TV series began with a kaleidoscope of big, brassy, sexy images – tracts of open land, shiny skyscrapers, fancy cars, cowboy businessmen and the very dreamy Victoria Principal ...
>
> A few years later, when I got to America on a college scholarship, I realized that the real American Dream was somewhat different from *Dallas*. I visited college friends in their hometowns and was struck by the spacious suburban houses and the gleaming appliances – even when their parents had simple, modest jobs. The modern American Dream, for me, was this general prosperity and well-being for the average person. European civilization had produced the great cathedrals of the world. America had the two-car garage. And this middle-class contentment created a country of optimists.[3]

Writing in *Time* (Thursday, 21st October) and rerunning the theme on CNN (5th February, 2011) Zarakia notes the angry and dispirited mood of America who, after the worst recession since the Great Depression, are strikingly fatalistic about their prospects. The middle class has been hollowed out and American workers are losing jobs as America companies locate off shore. The American Dream can be restored, Zakaria argues, but it will involve hard and painful choices and he makes the following recommendations: shift from consumption to investment; invest heavily in education and training; develop 'fiscal sanity'; and simplify the tax code and benchmark. He goes on to argue:

> My proposals are inherently difficult because they ask the left and right to come together, cut some spending, pare down entitlements, open up immigration for knowledge workers, rationalize the tax code – and then make large investments in education and training, research and technology, innovation and infrastructure. But the fact that it is a solution that crosses political borders should make it more palatable, not less. And time is crucial.

Zakaria buys into the concept of the American Dream without scrutinizing or historicizing it and the way it has changed and been narratively re-crafted for every age:

> That dream or hope has been present from the start. Ever since we became an independent nation, each generation has seen an uprising of ordinary Americans to save the American Dream from the forces which appear to be overwhelming it.

Yet with all narratives of this kind that serve as a basis of a national ideal and spell out an appeal to the better nature of citizens to unify them by alluding to a vision we need to ask what is the history of the narrative, who are the main story tellers and to what ends do they tell the tale? When we ask these questions the American Dream seems a very White dream, one that does not recognize how the dream rested on exploitation of indigenous peoples, the Black slave economy, and

Figure 20.

a corporate America that increasingly squeezes wealth from the American people and exploits cheap labor elsewhere in developing countries. While it is based on an ideal of inclusiveness it never offered indigenous peoples or Afro-Americans much hope.

THE EPIC OF AMERICA

James Truslow Adams was the historian who first coined the term 'American Dream' in *The epic of America* published in 1931, significantly at a time when America was suffering the early years of the Great Depression. He chose his title well. The term 'epic' is a long narrative poem detailing the heroic deeds and events significant to a culture, tribe or nation. In archaic Greek style these poems followed a certain format, exhibiting set literary conventions that described a heroic quest, normally beginning with an invocation to the muse, where genealogies are given and the values of a civilization are heralded. Homer's *Iliad* and *Odyssey* are classic examples that begin the Western tradition. These epics were often long national poems that described and embroidered the development of episodes or events important to the history of a nation or race told in an elevated style. It is a form that persists through the medieval into the modern era.

To describe America as an epic is to make appeal to noble sentiments and Adams was aware of this especially in the context of the 1930s he wanted to highlight and romanticize the ethic of equality and in particular, equality of opportunity and equality before the law. He also wanted to use these ideals and principles to describe a country based on the conscious development of a secular social order that found its origins in the Declaration of Independence which holds held certain truths to be self-evident: 'that all Men are created equal, that they are endowed by their Creator with certain unalienable Rights, that among these are Life, Liberty and the Pursuit of Happiness'. But do epics make good history and is the American Dream is still an attainable and serviceable ideal?

Adams was an historian who depicted a

dream of a land in which life should be better and richer and fuller for everyone, with opportunity for each according to ability or achievement. It is a difficult dream for the European upper classes to interpret adequately, and too many of us ourselves have grown weary and mistrustful of it. It is not a dream of motor cars and high wages merely, but a dream of social order in which each man and each woman shall be able to attain to the fullest stature of which they are innately capable, and be recognized by others for what they are, regardless of the fortuitous circumstances of birth or position. (pp. 214-215)

Adams was a writer rather than an academic and as a freelance writer he wrote colonial histories. His trilogy on the history of New England was warmly received and he won the Pulitzer Prize for the first volume, *The founding of New England* (1921). He was active in the American Society of Arts and Letters and various historical societies. In his *The epic of America* (1931), Adams attempted to address the historic development and philosophic vision of America that strongly reflected the values of the Declaration as uniquely American and extolled the advantages of education as a means for the promoting of equality of opportunity, meritocracy and social mobility. When he wrote *The epic of American* while living in London there was 16% unemployed – some eight million Americans – and unemployment was to get much worse as the depression dragged on. He died disappointed in his country after a heart attack in 1949.

Jim Cullen (2003) historicizes the American Dream focusing on the founding fathers and the Declaration of Independence as 'the charter of the American Dream', Abraham Lincoln and his dream for a unified nation as well as Martin Luther King Jr.'s dream of racial equality. He argues that the contemporary version of the American Dream has become debased built on its outlandish dreams of overnight fame and fortune. Perhaps most significantly, Cullen sees the American Dream as embodying the ideal that all men are created equal. Even with the obvious contradiction of slavery, the essence of this dream allowed for the possibility of racial equality, class mobility, and home ownership – values that are part of the core of collective consciousness of Americans.

Like Adams, Cullen deplores the way the American Dream increasingly become the pursuit of material prosperity and consumerism. David Camp (2009) suggests that while it matured into a shared dream under Roosevelt's New Deal where a new level of security that was cemented in place by The Social Security Act of 1935,[4] it was recalibrated during the period of postwar prosperity:

Buttressed by postwar optimism and prosperity, the American Dream was undergoing another recalibration. Now it really did translate into specific goals rather than Adams's more broadly defined aspirations. Home ownership was the fundamental goal, but, depending on who was doing the dreaming, the package might also include car ownership, television ownership (which multiplied from 6 million to 60 million sets in the U.S. between 1950 and 1960), and the intent to send one's kids to college. The G.I. Bill was as crucial on that last count as it was to the housing boom. In providing tuition money for returning vets, it not only stocked the universities with new students – in 1947, roughly half of the nation's

Figure 21.

college enrollees were ex-G.I'.s – but put the very idea of college within reach of a generation that had previously considered higher education the exclusive province of the rich and the extraordinarily gifted. Between 1940 and 1965, the number of U.S. adults who had completed at least four years of college more than doubled.

This was an ideal that translated the American Dream into a new society based upon purchasing power epitomized by John Kenneth Galbraith's (1958) *The afflu-ent society*, focusing on attaining hitherto undreamed levels of personal affluence. The succeeding decades exposed a commitment to high levels of personal debt via new credit cards, easy credit, and family investment portfolios in the bull markets of the day. At the same time the American Dream was being drained of its substantive content and 'decoupled from any concept of the common good (the movement to privatize Social Security began to take on momentum) and, more portentously, from the concepts of working hard and managing one's expectations'. As he goes on to comment:

> These are tough times for the American Dream. As the safe routines of our lives have come undone, so has our characteristic optimism – not only our belief that the future is full of limitless possibility, but our faith that things will eventually return to normal, whatever "normal" was before the recession hit. There is even worry that the dream may be over – that we currently living Americans are the unfortunate ones who shall bear witness to that deflating moment in history when the promise of this country began to wither. This is the "sapping of confidence" that President Obama alluded to in his inaugural address, the "nagging fear that America's decline is inevitable, and that the next generation must lower its sights".

As Hanson and Zogby (2010) suggest 'Cullen (2003) and others (Sherraden, 1991; Newman, 1993; Shapiro, 2004; Moen & Roehling, 2005; Johnson, 2006; Ho, 2007) have suggested that the American Dream may be unraveling as we see a growing wealth gap, ongoing race and gender inequality, and expanding poor immigrant populations. Perhaps the 21st century is not a time of increasing progress toward the American Dream'.

OBAMA ON THE AMERICAN DREAM

Barack Obama is a brilliant politician who knows the currency and power of the concept of 'American Dream'. His second book entitled *The audacity of hope* (2006) was subtitled *Thoughts on reclaiming the American Dream.*

> Most Americans have simple dreams. A job that can support a family. Health care we can count on and afford. A retirement that is dignified and secure. Education and opportunity for our kids. But today, the price of the American dream is going up. All across the country, Americans are working harder for less. We've never paid more for health care or for college. It's harder to save, and it's harder to retire. There are things we need to do right now to give our economy a boost, but a short-term stimulus is not enough. We have to put the American dream on a firmer foundation.

His recipe was clear: 'stop giving tax breaks to companies that ship jobs overseas, and to put a tax cut in the pocket of middle class Americans'; 'protect a secure retirement by easing the burden on America's seniors'; 'change our bankruptcy laws to protect workers' pensions instead of protecting banks'; 'make health care affordable and accessible for all Americans'. He wrote: 'We also have to be clear that the American dream must never come at the expense of the American family'. He also indicated the 'need to expand paid leave' and, perhaps most fundamentally, 'It's time to put a college education within reach of every American'.

The book became a national bestseller in the fall of 2006 and its promises and policy sketches became part of his 2008 campaign for the presidency. The phrase 'the audacity of hope' was one adopted from his pastor Jeremiah Wright (the audacity *to* hope) and Obama used it as the basis also for his keynote at the 2004 democratic convention.[5] In that speech he began by recalling his grandfather's dream and his family heritage to say:

> I stand here today, grateful for the diversity of my heritage, aware that my parents' dreams live on in my precious daughters. I stand here knowing that my story is part of the larger American story, that I owe a debt to all of those who came before me, and that, in no other country on earth, is my story even possible.

In the same paragraph Obama then alludes to the Declaration as a basis for the American Dream: 'We hold these truths to be self-evident, that all men are created equal. That they are endowed by their Creator with certain inalienable rights. That among these are life, liberty and the pursuit of happiness'. And he goes on to say: 'That is the true genius of America, a faith in the simple dreams of its people, the insistence on small miracles' and ends his speech with his own version of the Dream:

> I believe we can give our middle class relief and provide working families with a road to opportunity. I believe we can provide jobs to the jobless, homes to the homeless, and reclaim young people in cities across America from violence and despair. I believe that as we stand on the crossroads of history, we can make the right choices, and meet the challenges that face us. America!

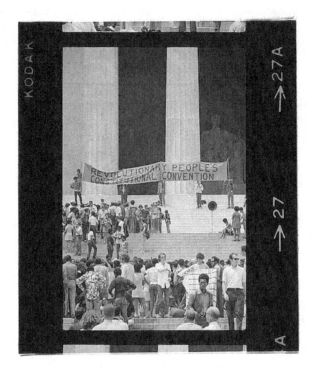

Figure 22.

In his postelection travels, Obama listened to a 30-year-old law school graduate who said he is no longer able to make the interest payments on his educational loans, much less able to have a mortgage or a family. He said he had been inspired by Obama's campaign. But now, 'that inspiration is dying away', he said 'I really want to know: Is the American Dream dead?' Obama responded: 'Absolutely not … There is not a country in the world that would want to change places with us', Obama responded. 'We are still the country that billions of people in the world look to and aspire to'.

'It's like the American Dream in reverse'. That's how President Barack Obama, ten days after taking office, described the plight of Americans hit by the faltering economy. His catchy description fell short – the Dream has turned into a nightmare for tens of millions.

Opinion polls reveal that increasingly Americans believe that 'the American Dream' is a thing of the past. Perhaps surprisingly, Hanson and Zogby (2010) report the majority of Americans consistently reported that the American Dream is more about spiritual happiness than material goods. Americans continue to believe that working hard is the most important element for getting ahead in the United States does not guarantee success. A majority of respondents believe that achieving the American Dream will be more difficult for future generations. Americans are increasingly pessimistic about the opportunity for the working class to get ahead

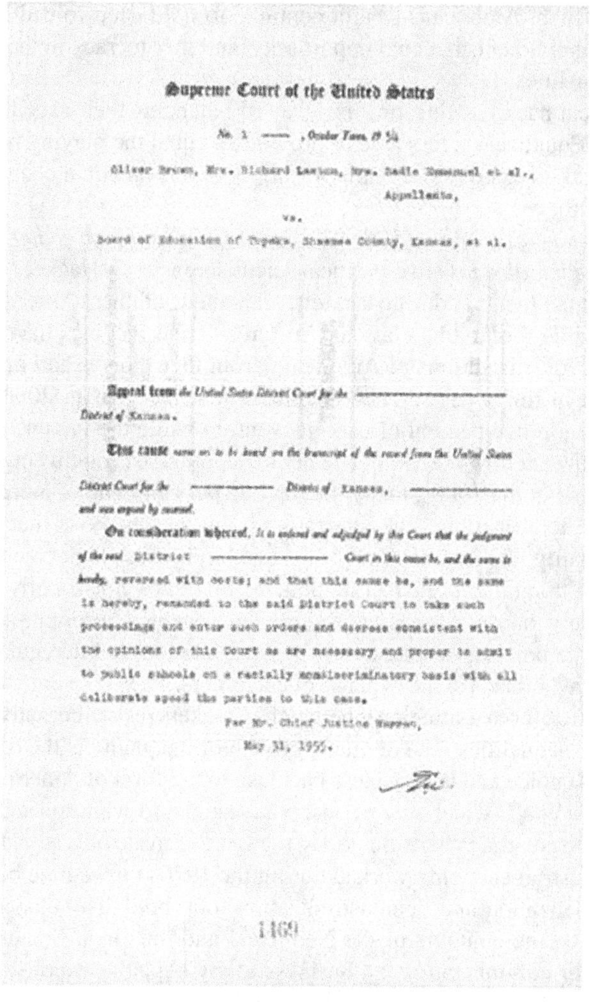

Supreme Court of the United States

No. 1 ——, October Term, 19 54

Oliver Brown, Mrs. Richard Lawton, Mrs. Sadie Emmanuel et al.,
Appellants,

vs.

Board of Education of Topeka, Shawnee County, Kansas, et al.

Appeal from the United States District Court for the ——— District of Kansas.

This cause came on to be heard on the transcript of the record from the United States District Court for the ——— District of Kansas, ——— and was argued by counsel.

On consideration whereof, It is ordered and adjudged by this Court that the judgment of the said District ——— Court in this cause be, and the same is hereby, reversed with costs; and that this cause be, and the same is hereby, remanded to the said District Court to take such proceedings and enter such orders and decrees consistent with the opinions of this Court as are necessary and proper to admit to public schools on a racially nondiscriminatory basis with all deliberate speed the parties to this case.

Per Mr. Chief Justice Warren,

May 31, 1955.

1469

Figure 23.

and increasingly optimistic about the opportunity for the poor and immigrants to get ahead in the United States.

As Hanson and Zogby (2010) comment 'Beliefs about opportunity are essential aspects of social systems in that they involve subjective interpretations of the legitimacy and openness of the stratification system … In the United States, there is considerable evidence that systems and structures work to the distinct advantage of some and to the disadvantage of others'. Obviously, growing and structured inequality is not compatible with the American Dream as its main ideological tenet is to suggest that all can succeed. In this context inequality is immoral and irresponsible. The American dream has been eclipsed by the power of wealth and the racial wealth gap is growing with generational inequality becoming even more deeply entrenched. Americans cannot continue to hold deep-rooted beliefs in the principles of individualism, equal opportunity, and meritocracy in the face of such growing inequalities.

As states cut back on education as a way of balancing their accounts education as the 'Great Equalizer' is less able to provide an equal the playing field, ensuring that every child – regardless of family of origin – gets an equal chance at success (Johnson, 2006).

In *Winner-take-all politics: How Washington made the rich richer – and turned its back on the middle class* two political scientists Jacob S. Hacker and Paul Pierson document the fact that during last few years the wealthiest Americans have got a lot richer while the middle class has suffered – real incomes have fallen, foreclosures have forced millions of Americans from their homes and unemployment is the highest in thirty years. They document that fact that in 2009 the average income of the top five percent of earners went up while the income of the rest of the population went down. The top one per cent possessed roughly eight percent of the total income in the 1960s; today the top one per cent 'earns' more than twenty percent of the total income. The interesting point they make is that this startling income inequality, the largest of any advanced industrial democracy, is part of a larger 40-year trend due to deliberate policies that have consistently cut taxes for the rich, made it harder for unions to organize, enabled corporations to pay top executives large bonuses despite company performance, and deregulated financial markets that favor banks at the expense of customers. They also point to intentional 'policy drift' to refer to a situation where policy makers resist alternatives that might have reduced inequalities. The dramatic growth of inequality is the result of deliberate political choice and the business backlash to the form of American liberalism emerging after WWII which saw a conservative counterrevolution and the political awakening of business. Where the policy regime of private provision for a globally dominant industrial economy worked during the 1970s this regime began to break down as globalization and deindustrialization took hold. The business lobby no longer accepted the contours of the New Deal and the Great Society. Beginning with the Carter administration the business lobby began to exercise their muscle defeating reform proposals and instituting a round of tax cuts.

During the 1960s and 1970s increasingly the parties differed on racial politics. The Republicans became the party of the wealthy and White while the Democrats became the inheritors of the civil rights movement. If anything this deep racial divide has grown larger during Obama's era exposing increasing racial inequalities which are likely to become even more pronounced as states begin to trim their budgets and cut back savagely into education and welfare entitlements. Under state budget cuts students have lost tuition waivers, teachers have been sacked, collective bargaining is curtailed and sometimes abolished, and deep cuts have been made to the funding of K-12 and higher education.[6]

Can education continue to play the role as the Great Equalizer sustaining the American Dream and providing the key to equality of opportunity?[7] Arne Duncan (2011), the Secretary of Education in the Obama administration, addressed the theme of education reform in the US in a series of remarks to the World Bank.

In his remarks he comments on the traditional values of education as the 'great equalizer' and its new role in the competitive knowledge economy of developing human capital:

> Education is now the key to eliminating gender inequality, to reducing poverty, to creating a sustainable planet, to preventing needless deaths and illness, and to fostering peace. And in a knowledge economy, education is the new currency by which nations maintain economic competitiveness and global prosperity. Education today is inseparable from the development of human capital.[8]

In his report of U.S. reforms he rejects the notion that improving economic competitiveness is a zero-sum game and in effect loads education with even more responsibility for 'achieving America' as Rorty puts it. Improving education is important to 'winning the future' he suggests, quoting President Obama. He also quotes with approval Thomas Friedman, Nelson Mandela ('Education is the most powerful weapon which you can use to change the world') and Ben Bernanke ('the best solution to income inequality is producing a high-quality education for everyone'). And he puts the point in graphic terms:

> We have more than two million children enrolled in preschool programs, 100,000 public schools, 49 million K-12 students, more than three million teachers, and 15,000 school districts – all of it largely administered and funded by local governments. I am convinced that the U.S. education system now has an unprecedented opportunity to get dramatically better. Nothing – nothing – is more important in the long-run to American prosperity than boosting the skills and attainment of the nation's students. In the United States, we feel an economic and moral imperative to challenge the status quo. Closing the achievement gap and closing the opportunity gap is the civil rights issue of our generation. One quarter – 25 percent – of U.S. high school students drop out or fail to graduate on time. Almost one million students leave our schools for the streets each year. That is economically unsustainable and morally unacceptable.

If 'the economic future of the United States rests on its ability to strengthen our education system' then in the current situation with state-led budget cuts and the general recession the American Dream is severely at risk. The authors of *The global auction* (Brown, Lauder, & Ashton, 2011) suggest that in a more integrated and networked world the market value of American workers is no longer a national matter, but rather is part of a global auction for jobs. They challenge the conventional wisdom that more education will lead to greater individual and national prosperity that has been a cornerstone of developed economies arguing that globalization has led to new global high-skill, low-wage workforce. Their work not only questions the easy adoption of education as human capital development but calls for a radical questioning of education as the principal mechanism for the achievement of the American Dream.

NOTES

[1] For the full speech and video see http://www.huffingtonpost.com/2008/03/18/obama-race-speech-read-th_n_92077.html.

[2] See Rorty's (1999) *Philosophy and social hope* that represents his hope for 'a global cosmopolitan, democratic, egalitarian, classless, casteless society' (p. xii) and runs this hope together with his antagonism towards Platonism – towards the search for Truth (as correspondence), certainty, reality and essences. He finds the roots of his view in the work of the American native tradition in pragmatist philosophy best represented in the work of John Dewey.

[3] http://www.time.com/time/nation/article/0,8599,2026776,00.html#ixzz1FYWfxQRo.

[4] See the wonderful set of photos that accompanies this article at http://www.vanityfair.com/culture/features/2009/04/american-dream200904?currentPage=1.

[5] For the full speech see http://www.librarian.net/dnc/speeches/obama.txt.

[6] See the report from the Center on Budget and Policy Priorities on State budget cuts at http://www.cbpp.org/cms/index.cfm?fa=view&id=1214. Jerry Brown in California aims to cut half a billion dollars from state education funding in 2011; Arizona \$83.7 million; Georgia \$187 from higher education; Texas, \$5 billion from public schools; and so on. In a much publicized episode Gov. Scott Walker of Wisconsin in the largest cut in modern state history has cut \$900 million in aid to school districts (also preventing any rise in property taxes) and eliminated collective bargaining rights of state employees, leading to historic protests against him. See the full text of his budget speech at http://walker.wi.gov/journal_media_detail.asp?prid=5668&locid=177 and the senate Bill at http://legis.wisconsin.gov/2011/data/JR1SB-11.pdf.

[7] See Bill Gates' (2011) Ted Talk on 'How State Budgets are breaking US schools' at http://www.ted.com/talks/bill_gates_how_state_budgets_are_breaking_us_schools.html.

[8] See his 'Improving human capital in a competitive world – Education reform in the United States', remarks of U.S. Secretary of Education, Arne Duncan, World Bank, Human Development Network Forum, March 2, 2011 at http://web.worldbank.org/WBSITE/EXTERNAL/NEWS/0,,contentMDK:22848251~pagePK:34370~piPK:42770~theSitePK:4607,00.html.

REFERENCES

Brown, Phillip, Lauder, Hugh, & Aston (2011). *The global auction: The broken promises of education, jobs, and incomes.* Oxford: Oxford University Press.

Cullen, James (2003). *The American Dream: A short history of an idea that shaped a nation.* New York: Oxford University Press.

Hacker, Jacob S. & Pierson, Paul (2010). *Winner-take-all politics: How Washington made the rich richer – and turned its back on the middle class.* New York: Simon & Schuster.

Hanson, S.L. & Zogby, J. (Fall 2010). The polls – trends; Attitudes about the American Dream, *Public Opinion Quarterly, 74*(3), 570-584.

Ho, Alfred K. (2007). *Achieving the American Dream.* Lanham, MD: Hamilton Books.

Hochschild, Jennifer L. (1995). *Facing up to the American Dream: Race, class, and the soul of the nation.* Princeton, NJ: Princeton University Press.

Johnson, H.B. (2006). *The American Dream and the power of wealth: Choosing schools and inheriting inequality in the land of opportunity.* New York: Routledge.

Kamp, David (April 2009). Rethinking the American Dream, *Vanity Fair,* http://www.vanityfair.com/culture/features/2009/04/american-dream200904. Retrieved June 20, 2009.

Newman, Katherine S. (1993). *Declining fortunes: The withering of the American Dream.* New York: Basic Books.

Rorty, Richard (1998). *Achieving our country: Leftist thought in twentieth-century America.* Cambridge, MA: Harvard University Press.

Shapiro, Thomas M. (2004). *The hidden cost of being African American: How wealth perpetuates inequality.* New York: Oxford University Press.

EPILOGUE

The Dream of Global Educational Equality

We are such stuff
As dreams are made on; and our little life
Is rounded with a sleep.

Shakespeare, *The Tempest* Act 4, scene 1, 148-158

I say to you today, my friends, that in spite of the difficulties and frustrations of the moment, I still have a dream. It is a dream deeply rooted in the American dream. I have a dream that one day this nation will rise up and live out the true meaning of its creed: "We hold these truths to be self-evident: that all men are created equal".

Martin Luther King, *Delivered on the steps at the Lincoln Memorial in Washington D.C. on August 28, 1963*

One of the two major features of this short book has been the emphasis on the epic form of narrative with which to cast ideals and enduring values as part of a noble vision that become the American Dream; the other is the essential significance of the value of equality, especially in relation to education that permits informed citizenship within a democracy and also enables personal and collective betterment and generational progress towards a society that embodies these ideals more perfectly. Neither feature I would argue is specifically American although the history of America and the unfolding of the history of the future gives the Dream and its underlying values a cultural specificity. Philosophers, politicians and historians like Rorty, Obama, and Adams have each sought to focus on the American specificity of the Dream by emphasizing elements of political philosophy and cultural history that are unique to America, yet I would argue that now it is time to understand the wider sources for the Dream of Equality, its prehistory before the birth of America and its global basis for world history. Only the global dream of equality can help America sustain itself, its values and institutions. The success of the Dream today is the extent to which it is adopted, adapted and defined elsewhere, and in this context we need to become more aware of the medium of the Dream, its narrative development, and the history of equality. The dream of equality and its representation go hand in hand.

Nowhere is the epic form of narrative more open to genre and media development than in the USA with its new vital democratic and open web 2.0 technologies

Figure 24.

that has the communicational and cinematic possibilities of depicting the Dream in ways undreamed of by the founders of the constitution. Shakespeare was, of course, not the first dramatist to make use of dreams. Greek tragedy and the epics of Horace and Virgil contained useful models for connecting the dream with an event to come, for which the dream paved the way in an allegorical sense. A dream is in some ways involuntary, as a succession of ideas, images and emotions, yet many cultures have sought meaning in dreams, sometimes in spiritual terms and often in subconscious terms. Dreams have been considered prophetic or messages from the divine. Evolutionary psychologists suggest that dreams provide some survival function. They were used historically as a source of healing and guidance and in modern psychotherapy as a projection of self, especially those parts that have been ignored or overlooked. In *The interpretation of dreams*, Freud tells us that in ancient times dreams were consider being of divine inspiration sent to the dreamer to foretell the future or to misguide and lead the dreamer to destruction. Famously, he defines the dream in terms of 'wish fulfillment'.[1] In popular culture, dreams are often seen as the source of our deepest fears and desires. In literary form the dream vision narrative has constituted a genre that embraces poetry, drama, romance, lyric and didactic forms like the sermon. Visionary literature can contain elements of all these components as well as the historical, the theological and the philosophical. Old English literature consists in epic poetry, hagiography, sermons, chronicles and Bible translations. I began with Shakespeare because he more than any other is responsible for expanding and shaping the dramatic representation of dreams, using them throughout his oeuvre and invoking the classical conception of dreams as a premonition of the future.

The speech by Martin Luther King, Jr., 'I Had a Dream',[2] delivered on August 28, 1963 from the steps of the Lincoln Memorial to 200,000 supporters, called for racial equality and an end to discrimination. It was a defining moment of the American civil rights movement. 'I have a dream' is repeated in eight successive sentences and in conjunction with the word 'freedom' which is repeated twenty times. It evokes a set of powerful historic and literary references to Lincoln's Gettysburg Address, to the Declaration of Independence, and to the Bible. It makes reference to the geography of the civil rights movement – to Mississippi, to Alabama, to the South. The 17 minute speech is divided into two parts: the first half depicts the nightmare of racial injustice in America and the second half pictures a dream of racial harmony. Some scholars argue that stylistically the speech resemble a Baptist sermon; others see the speech as a political treatise or a work of poetry. The dream of equality and the American Dream became one in the skillful rhetoric of Obama.

The history of equality from antiquity onward reveals that the notion of equality has been considered a constitutive feature of justice whether in its formal, proportional, or moral sense. We must remember that until the eighteenth century human beings were considered unequal by nature, an idea that collapsed with the introduction of the notion of natural right first developed by the Stoics and later in the New Testament Bible and both the Hebraic and Islamic traditions. The principle of natural equality only became recognized in the modern period beginning in the seventeenth century in the tradition of natural law as defined by Hobbes and Locke, and in social contract theory first postulated by Rousseau. Kant's categorical imperative formulates the equality postulate of universal human worth and the idea is taken up formally in declarations and modern constitutions, notably the French Declaration of the Rights of Man and of the Citizen (1789) (*Déclaration des droits de l'Homme et du Citoyen*)[3], the American Declaration of Independence[4] (1776), The US Constitution[5] (1787), and the Universal Declaration of Human Rights[6] (1948). As Stefan Gosepath (2007) explains 'This fundamental idea of equal respect for all persons and of the equal worth or equal dignity of all human beings ... is accepted as a minimal standard by all leading schools of modern Western political and moral culture'. It has not always been so.

The landmark U.S. Supreme Court decision of May 17, 1954, Brown v. the Board of Education was a turning point for the US. The case initiated the modern civil rights movement. Chief Justice Warren delivered the opinion of the court: 'We come then to the question presented: Does segregation of children in public schools solely on the basis of race, even though the physical facilities and other "tangible" factors may be equal, deprive the children of the minority group of equal educational opportunities? We believe that it does ... We conclude that in the field of public education the doctrine of "separate but equal" has no place. Separate educational facilities are inherently unequal'. And he prefaces his opinion with the following statement:

Today, education is perhaps the most important function of state and local governments. Compulsory school attendance laws and the great expenditures for education both demonstrate our recognition of the importance of education to our democratic society. It is required in the performance of our most basic public responsibilities, even service in the armed forces. It is the very foundation of good citizenship. Today it is a principal instrument in awakening the child to cultural values, in preparing him for later professional training, and in helping him to adjust normally to his environment. In these days, it is doubtful that any child may reasonably be expected to succeed in life if he is denied the opportunity of an education. Such an opportunity, where the state has undertaken to provide it, is a right which must be made available to all on equal terms.[7]

As the Brown Foundation website summary makes clear: 'From the earliest times in American history, the U.S. educational system mandated separate schools for children based solely on race. In many instances, the schools for African American children were substandard facilities with out-of-date textbooks and insufficient supplies'. The first documented school desegregation case goes back to 1849 (Roberts vs. City of Boston).[8] Yet as James D. Anderson (2004, p. 359) 'A half century after the U.S. Supreme Court found that segregated schools are inherently unequal, there is growing evidence that the nation's public schools are becoming more segregated and that academic achievement is becoming more unequal'. He concludes with the comment: 'The promises of *Brown* are unfulfilled, and the nation has to face up to this reality. Let us not evade the problems by making African Americans the scapegoats for the nation's failure and giving them yet another cross to bear' (p. 371). His early work examines the ideological and institutional nature of schooling in the black South detailing the fact that 'former slaves were the first among native southerners to depart from the planters' ideology of education and society and to campaign for universal, state-supported public education' (Anderson, 1988, p. 4).

The dream of educational equality was incorporated into early prototypes of the Declaration of the Rights of man and of the Citizen. Bergström (2010) indicates the right to education is seen as a second-generation right developing when social rights became prominent in the second half of the nineteenth century ... first in national normative instruments and later, in the second half of the twentieth century, in international declarations and conventions'. Gill (2010) explains that:

in the sixteenth and seventeenth centuries, most educational works were still either practical manuals addressed to parents and concerned primarily with the communication of received wisdom and the teaching of manners, or they were specialized texts that put forth new methods of forming the mind. The late seventeenth and early eighteenth century witnessed the birth of a more ambitious project: the educational treatise, in which reformers took on the task of translating theory into practice, applying new philosophical ideas directly to techniques of child-rearing.

Yet it is the case that equality was an early theme in the eighteenth century especially in relation to education developed most significantly by Rousseau on *The discourse on inequality* (orig. 1754) where he believed he had traced,

the origin and progress of inequality, and the institution and abuse of political societies, as far as these are capable of being deduced from the nature of man merely by the light of reason, and independently of those sacred dogmas which give the sanction of divine right to sovereign authority.

On this basis he maintained that 'there is hardly any inequality in the state of nature, all the inequality which now prevails owes its strength and growth to the development of our faculties and the advance of the human mind, and becomes at last permanent and legitimate by the establishment of property and laws' and he suggested:

> it follows that moral inequality, authorised by positive right alone, clashes with natural right, whenever it is not proportionate to physical inequality; a distinction which sufficiently determines what we ought to think of that species of inequality which prevails in all civilised countries; since it is plainly contrary to the law of nature, however defined, that children should command old men, fools wise men, and that the privileged few should gorge themselves with superfluities, while the starving multitude are in want of the bare necessities of life.

Chisnik (1991) has documented the fact that there was ambivalence or contradiction in the idea of equality in the French Enlightenment that on the one hand asserted equality and only to specify its practical limit on the other. He explains 'this contradiction in terms of the context in which the idea of equality was discussed and the purpose it was intended to serve' (p. 215) arguing:

> We find, then, that Jaucourt, Robinet and Voltaire – and we might well include Bastide – all on the one hand admit the original or natural equality of men, while on the other, they deny this natural equality practical application. (p. 218)

In passing he notes that the,

> American statement on the primal equality of men was written by an owner of slaves and was accepted by many others who also owned slaves, and who saw no incongruity in maintaining both the principle of natural equality and their property in human beings. With respect to the French document, Georges Lefebvre, following Aulard, has pointed out that it was essentially negative in purport, its main purpose being to deny the principal values of the old regime. (p. 220)

It is a source of ambiguity that has endured until today as Christopher Jencks (1988, p. 518) points out by analytically providing five conceptions of equal educational opportunity 'each of which draws on a different tradition and each of which has different practical consequences':

1. *Democratic equality*. Democratic equality requires ... [the teacher] to give everyone equal time and attention, regardless of how well they read, how hard they try, how deprived they have been in the past, what they want, or how much they or others will benefit.
2. *Moralistic justice*. Moralistic justice requires ... [the teacher] to reward virtue and punish vice. In the classroom, virtue involves effort, and moralistic justice means rewarding those who make the most effort to learn whatever [the teacher] is trying to teach.
3. *Weak humane justice*. Since some students have gotten less than their proportionate share of advantages in the past, humane justice requires [the teacher] to compensate those students by giving them more than their proportionate share of her attention while they are in her classroom. But the "weak" variant of humane justice only requires [the teacher] to compensate those who have been shortchanged at home or in their earlier schooling, not those who have been shortchanged genetically.

4. *Strong humane justice*. This variant of humane justice requires [the teacher] to compensate those who have been shortchanged in *any* way in the past, including genetically. In practice, this means giving the most attention to the worst readers, regardless of the reasons for their illiteracy.

5. *Utilitarianism*. Most utilitarians assume that the best way to get individuals to do what we want is to make every activity, including education, a race for unequal rewards. Equal opportunity means that such races must be open to all, run on a level field, and judged solely on the basis of performance. Thus, insofar as [the teacher's] attention is a prize, it should go to the best readers. (pp. 520-521).

The analytical picture is further complicated by the history of equality as it emerges in the contested view of the Enlightenment by liberal historians and philosophers on the one hand and Nietzschean inspired critics on the other. Stuurman (2010) provides the relevant observation:

In the dominant canon of history and politics in the West, the Enlightenment is depicted as the historical moment that laid the groundwork for today's hegemonic global culture of liberal democracy and human rights ... According to the postmodern critics, the Enlightenment tenet of improving the human condition according to a rational design led to the colonial project of a "civilizing mission", and finally to the ghastly utopianisms of the totalitarian ideologies of the twentieth century.

It may be the case that that the notion of equality is open to conflicting interpretations (what concept isn't) and that the history of the Enlightenment is not the unblemished noble epic of Western civilization (here Nietzsche teaches us about the illusions of monumental history[9]). Nevertheless, in this imperfect world the values that were struck during the Enlightenment, even in their conflicted form, formed the basis of a political culture that offers a dream of human betterment based on formal and moral notions of equality. This dream has a certain distinctive history and trajectory in America but it is not exclusively an American Dream nor should it be so considered. Indeed, if anything the notion of equality in whatever form cannot be theorized to apply only to a select group of people – Americans. If it has any moral or political force we must act and think on the premise that it applies to everyone everywhere; and that is the global challenge to the American Dream.

NOTES

[1] See the full text version at http://www.bartleby.com/285/ (III. The Dream is the Fulfilment of a Wish).

[2] For the text, audio and video and see http://www.americanrhetoric.com/speeches/mlkihaveadream.htm.

[3] For the full text, see http://www.hrcr.org/docs/frenchdec.html

[4] For the full text, see http://www.usconstitution.net/declar.html.

[5] For the full text, see http://www.usconstitution.net/const.html.

 For the full text see http://www.un.org/en/documents/udhr/index.shtml.

 For the full text of the opinion, see http://brownvboard.org/content/opinion-brown-347us483.

 See http://brownvboard.org/content/background-overview-summary.

 See Nietzsche's 'On the use and abuse of history for life' at http://records.viu.ca/~johnstoi/ nietzsche/history.htm.

REFERENCES

Anderson, James D. (1988). *The education of Blacks in the South, 1860-1935.* Chapel Hill, NC: University of North Carolina Press.

Anderson, James D. (July, 2004). Crosses to bear and promises to keep: The jubilee anniversary of *Brown v. Board of Education, Urban Education, 39*(4), 359-373. At http://www.wsu.edu/~dee/ENLIGHT/DISC2.htm.

Bergstrom, Y. (2010). The universal right to education: Freedom, equality and fraternity, *Stud. Philos. Educ., 29*, 167-182.

Chisnik, Harvey (1991). The ambivalence of the idea of equality in the French enlightenment, *History of European Ideas, 13*(3), 215-223.

Freud, Sigmund. (1900). *The interpretation of dreams.* Trans. by A.A. Brill (1913). New York: Macmillan.

Gill, Natasha (2010). *Educational philosophy in the French enlightenment: From nature to second nature.* London: Ashgate.

Jencks, Christopher (April, 1988). Whom must we treat equally for educational opportunity to be equal?, *Ethics, 98*(3), 518-533. http://links.jstor.org/sici?sici=0014-1704%28198804%2998%3A3%3C518%3AWMWTEF%3E2.0.CO%3B2-7.

Rousseau, Jean-Jacques (1754/1913). *The discourse on inequality.* Translated by G.D. Cole, in Jean-Jacques Rousseau, *The social contract and discourses* (pp. 207-238). London: J.M. Dent (1913).

Stuurman, Siep (2010). Global equality and inequality in enlightenment thought. At http://www.18e-eeuw.nl/symposia/stuurman.pdf.

TINA BESLEY

POSTSCRIPT

Education America – 'Welcome to My Nightmare'

Welcome to My Nightmare is the first track and name of a 1975 concept al-
bum by Alice Cooper has a sequence of songs that form a journey through
the nightmares of a child named Steven. Cooper sings "Welcome to my nightmare./Welcome to my breakdown./I hope I didn't scare you./That's just the way
we are/When we come down./We sweat, laugh and scream here,/Cuz life is just a
dream here" (from: http://www.elyrics.net/read/a/alice-cooper-lyrics/welcome-to-
my-nightmare-lyrics.html). The American Dream for many Americans has turned
into a nightmare, especially for the youth of America who are caught in a pin-
cer movement: automation has hollowed out the service sector, the sector with
greatest predicted job growth for the college educated; youth unemployment is
at a record high in the US and internationally approaching 50% in some nation-
states and cities[1]; the policy mantras suggest that higher education is the only
ticket to the knowledge economy yet the US states are attacking education, sacking
teachers and reducing education budgets, while universities are raising fees forcing
a privatization of student debt of historic proportions. Welcome to our nightmare!

Living in USA from 2005–2011, through the last part of President G.W. Bush's
second term and the first of President Barack Obama, has been to witness massive
changes in both the USA and the wider world once the global financial crisis im-
pacted and has continued being a festering sore. The ongoing debt crisis impacts not
only on USA but also on Europe with austerity budgets being introduced in most
locations, including an attack on education with increased student fees in Higher
Education.

It has meant that the USA's global position and consequently its confidence
in itself has been dented, temporarily at least. It has meant that the middle class
has borne much pain with the housing market crash, job losses, and loss of health
insurance. For the poor, the recession has meant a huge increase in those now below
the poverty line (15.1% in 2010, the highest since 1993, comprising 46.2 million
people) with a clear ethnic dimension, with current statistics showing how badly
affected are African Americans and Hispanics.[2]

For the rich, well they've done well, the richest 5% had their incomes surge 42%
from 1980. The recent 2011 Occupy Wall Street protests highlight the now well
known statistics of the wealthiest achieving substantial income growth such that
1% own and control resources in the U.S. compared with the rest of the population
(see http://www.cbo.gov/doc.cfm?index=12485). At a Joint Economic Committee

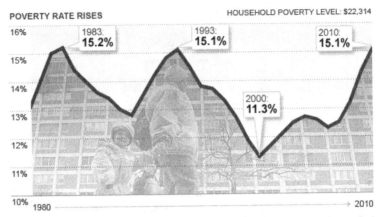

POVERTY RATE RISES | HOUSEHOLD POVERTY LEVEL: $22,314

Figure 25. Source: http://money.cnn.com/2011/09/13/news/economy/poverty_rate_income/index.htm

hearing, October 4, 2011, Federal Reserve Chairman Ben Bernanke said, "[P]eople are quite unhappy with the state of the economy and what's happening. They blame, with some justification, the problems in the financial sector for getting us into this mess, and they're dissatisfied with the policy response here in Washington. And at some level, I can't blame them. Certainly, 9 percent unemployment and very slow growth is not a good situation" (http://en.wikipedia.org/wiki/Occupy_Wall_Street). The protests, largely led by youth and others inspired by the Arab Spring and using social media to garner support, have spread to over 900 cities worldwide amid growing anger at the unethical behavior, lack of accountability and regulation of financial institutions.[3]

Democracy seems to be good at protest, but is it good at community building? The electoral processes and party politics in the current era in the USA do not seem to have any focus on community building, more on point scoring and destroying the opposition. The President is hamstrung by a structural system with supposed 'checks and balances' but which now sees little cross- party agreement on any-thing. Globalization has clearly benefitted the transnational companies, but not the nation state which is left struggling to find jobs for its people as the multinational corporations has re-located factories to wherever the labor rates and regulation are the least, especially to China, India, Vietnam, Mexico and soon probably to Africa. I can't help wonder if the society is in a process of cannibalizing itself, especially certain groups, in devouring the young, the poor, and people of color?

In Southern California in 2006–2008, I spent time with my students (who were doing Master Science in Educational Counseling) in many schools in different school districts (rich and poor) in the Inland Empire. I was struck by the way that some appeared more like prisons than schools – wire fences topped with barbed wire, police presence, onsite security and wondered how it made the young people feel about their school and education? Did it really made the kids feels safe? Not all schools were like this, nor were local universities (nor University of Illinois at Urbana Champaign); not those in relatively well-off Redlands and country areas which still had open grounds. I was surprised then to find the contrast of some

Annual U.S. income share of the Top 1%

Figure 26. Congressional Budget Office (CBO) data shows that in 1980, the top 1% earned 9.1% of all income, while in 2006 they earned 18.8% of all income Source: http://en.wikipedia.org/wiki/Occupy_Wall_Street.

new schools in seemingly well off areas of Palm Desert were such fortresses that I could not even access a staff/faculty toilet without a key. The point of the security was ostensibly to keep out all sorts of undesirable or 'bad' people, including gang members – all important considering the inter-gang tensions amid a plethora of guns, violence and local murders, so that students can feel they are in a safe physical environment. However, why did some schools not see this need? Why are some areas able to construct new schools once their existing ones reach a certain size, whereas in a neighboring school district enrolment has to be kept open despite reaching over 3300 students in their middle or high schools, since they can not afford to construct new schools? Why are schools funded so differently by different areas? There are many more questions, but such structural issues are ones that need to be addressed if America wants its children – its future, to be able to engage fully with the global knowledge economy. Should a child who lives in a district that is not able to take in as much local tax to fund schools as its neighboring district be provided with lesser educational resources? Is this the child's fault? What happened to the now quaint notion of 'equal educational opportunity'? What, if anything is being done to address this? In an austerity budgeting era, it seems to be off the radar.

When I return to the statements made in the heady days following Obama's election, I find the Obama-Biden Plan, from the Office of the President-Elect:

Barack Obama and Joe Biden believe that our kids and our country can't afford four more years of neglect and indifference. At this defining moment in our history, America faces few more urgent challenges than preparing our children

109

to compete in a global economy. The decisions our leaders make about education in the coming years will shape our future for generations to come. Obama and Biden are committed to meeting this challenge with the leadership and judgment that has been sorely lacking for the last eight years. Their vision for a 21st century education begins with demanding more reform and accountability, coupled with the resources needed to carry out that reform; asking parents to take responsibility for their children's success; and recruiting, retaining, and rewarding an army of new teachers to fill new successful schools that prepare our children for success in college and the workforce. The Obama–Biden plan will restore the promise of America's public education, and ensure that American children again lead the world in achievement, creativity and success. (http://change.gov/agenda/education_agenda/)

The Obama–Biden plan focus on reform and accountability seems to be more of the same neo-liberal critique of education. It holds a somewhat negative focus as its core rather than an actual positive move apart from more resources, nothing particularly innovative or creative changes. It lists three aspects for Early Childhood, twelve aspects for K-12 and two for Higher Education.[4] The formulation and implementation of such a plan is passed to US Department of Education and Education Secretary, Arne Duncan who in an interview with Charlie Rose in 2009, envisioned a

> public school becoming a community center, meaning that when he advocates the lengthening of the school day, he's not necessarily calling for more public money to be spent on after-school programs. But, literally, using the building as a community center. So private groups, like the Boys and Girls club or the YMCA would hold classes there; maybe private arts foundations would do the same and maybe these private groups would help pay for equipment they would need and the school could get the benefit. This, of course, is done in many communities at many schools on an ad hoc basis, but hasn't been part of a national mandate (cited by Chuck Todd, 2009, in http://firstread.msnbc.msn.com/_news/2009/03/12/4424745-understanding-obamas-education-vision)

Two years later, this seems to not have panned out, but remains a tantalising and perhaps a challenging vision.

Not surprisingly towards the end of his first term certain right wing commentators (e.g. Andrew Breitbart) criticise the Obama administration for spending without sufficient results: 'Despite a doubling in inflation-adjusted per-pupil spending since the early 1970s, student achievement is flat at best. While he brags constantly about his Race to the Top initiative, in which states competed for $4 billion to fund innovative programs, he's spent more than $80 billion in no-strings-attached stimulus funds to maintain the educational status quo"; for cutting 'a successful and popular DC that let low-income residents exercise the same choice Obama did in sending his daughters to private school' and for ongoing support of teacher unions, an important part of his support base. (http://biggovernment.com/reasontv/2010/10/09/3-reasons-obamas-education-vision-deserves-an-f/).

K-12 education and teaching and its funding have become a highly politicised, with left and right all holding strong opinions about the merits or otherwise of the system. The right argue that spending more is not making any significant difference in school level education, and then proceed to attack teacher unions and protectionism. The left argue for measures to address inequalities and in particular criticise the moves to promote Charter schools. In 2010–2011 however, we have seen teachers increasingly under attack – from conditions of work and negotiating issues to receiving 'pink slips' that indicate lay-offs. Larry Abramson, argues that laying off many especially newer teachers in spring and then re-hiring some but not all in Fall have become 'a way of life' (see Abramson, 2011, http://www.npr.org/2011/06/15/137090661/in-teaching-pink-slips-are-a-way-of-life). The job security of teachers in many states has come under serious threat. For example, in February 2011, according to Molly Line, school district leaders in Providence Rhode Island, in an 'unprecedented move to reduce spending and reign in a massive $40 million dollar budget shortfall' signalled a 'plan to send dismissal notices to every teacher in the district by March 1st, meeting a legal deadline to warn teachers of changes to their employment status' [some 2000 teachers] (Line, M., 2011, http://liveshots.blogs.foxnews.com/2011/02/24/providence-plans-to-pink-slip-all-teachers/#ixzz1evnTU63G). In March 14 2011, ABC News reported that 26,000 teachers in California received pink slips, while CBS reported a lower figure of 19,000 (http://abclocal.go.com/kabc/story?section=news/state&id=6710423; http://www.cbsnews.com/stories/2011/03/16/national/main20043778.shtml).

Comments such as 'In Teaching, Pink Slips Are a Way of Life', by Larry Abramson on National Public Radio in June 2011, highlight a growing problem amid the economic downturn. The article notes that the American Association of School Administrators has estimated that some 'quarter-million educators could face layoffs in the coming year as states cut education spending in an effort to balance their budgets'. The layoff notices usually have to be sent out in spring with such uncertainty a blow to teacher morale, and fears about future income, even though many may in fact be re-hired or 'recalled' over summer, and particularly impact on young an new teachers. (Abramson, 2011, http://www.npr.org/2011/06/15/137090661/in-teaching-pink-slips-are-a-way-of-life).

On February 11, 2011, Scott Walker, the new Republican Governor for Wisconsin set out a bill aimed at curbing a budget shortfall of $137 million for the fiscal year ending July 1, 2011, which Mary Bruce's report on ABC News indicated 'would strip workers of the right to bargain over anything other than wages, which could not rise faster than the Consumer Price Index. Teachers and other state workers would also no longer be able to negotiate for better pensions or health benefits.' Massive protests ensued but Walker prevailed. Similarly, she reports, New Jersey Republican Governor, Chris Christie made his attack on teacher unions clear, arguing that "We have built a system ... that cares more about the feelings of adults than the future of children", he said in a speech at the American Enterprise Institute in Washington, D.C. on Tuesday. "Tell me where else is there a profession with no reward for excellence and no penalty for failure?" (Bruce, 2011, http://abcnews.go.com/Politics/wisconsin-protests-news-wisconsin-governor-scott-walkers-proposal/story?id=12942012#.Tt7mtL8z3Zc).

In public Higher Education in USA, the field I was in for 6 years in USA after 5 years in Glasgow UK, budgetary issues have had serious impact on the funding of public universities in many states. For example, when I started at University of Illinois in 2005, the state funded almost half the university receipts, but by 2011, it was less than 20%. There are similar stories in other states, including Wisconsin and California especially at UC Berkeley and UCLA, highlighted by Reich's figures that follow. In the process public universities are becoming privatised by stealth, which is likely to see the reinstitution of class and wealth as key indicators for student intake, rather than merit.

Robert Reich's 2010, 'American Education under Attack' in *The Christian Science Monitor*, puts figures to the rhetoric. His summary statistics on cuts in state education follows and provide stern warnings arguing that such cuts 'seriously threaten the nation's future'. First he details pre-school & K-12 cuts as follows:

— Arizona has eliminated preschool for 4,328 children, funding for schools to provide additional support to disadvantaged children from preschool to third grade, aid to charter schools, and funding for books, computers, and other classroom supplies. The state also halved funding for kindergarten, leaving school districts and parents to shoulder the cost of keeping their children in school beyond a half-day schedule.

— California has reduced K-12 aid to local school districts by billions of dollars and is cutting a variety of programs, including adult literacy instruction and help for high-needs students.

— Colorado has reduced public school spending in FY 2011 by $260 million, nearly a 5 percent decline from the previous year. The cut amounts to more than $400 per student.

— Georgia has cut state funding for K-12 education for FY 2011 by $403 million or 5.5 percent relative to FY 2010 levels. The cut has led the state's board of education to exempt local school districts from class size requirements to reduce costs.

— Hawaii shortened the 2009–10 school year by 17 days and furloughed teachers for those days.

— Illinois has cut school education funding by $241 million or 3 percent in its FY 2011 budget relative to FY 2010 levels. Cuts include a significant reduction in funding for student transportation and the elimination of a grant program intended to improve the reading and study skills of at-risk students from kindergarten through the 6th grade.

— Maryland has cut professional development for principals and educators, as well as health clinics, gifted and talented summer centers, and math and science initiatives.

- Michigan has cut its FY 2010 school aid budget by $382 million, resulting in a $165 per-pupil spending reduction.
- Over the course of FY10, Mississippi cut by 7.2 percent funding for the Mississippi Adequate Education Program, a program established to bring per-pupil K-12 spending up to adequate levels in every district.
- Massachusetts has cut state education aid by $115.6 million, or 3 percent in its FY 2011 budget relative to FY 2010 levels. It also made a $4.6 million, or 16 percent cut relative to FY 2010 levels to funding for early intervention services, which help special-needs children develop appropriately and be ready for school.
- Missouri is cutting its funding for K-12 transportation by 46 percent. The cut in funding likely will lead to longer bus rides and the elimination of routes for some of the 565,000 students who rely on the school bus system.
- New Jersey has cut funding for afterschool programs aimed to enhance student achievement and keep students safe between the hours of 3 and 6 p.m. The cut will likely cause more than 11,000 students to lose access to the programs and 1,100 staff workers to lose their jobs.
- North Carolina cut by 21 percent funding for a program targeted at small schools in low-income areas and with a high need for social workers and nurses. As a result, 20 schools will be left without a social worker or nurse. The state also temporarily eliminated funding for teacher mentoring.
- Rhode Island cut state aid for K-12 education and reduced the number of children who can be served by Head Start and similar services.
- Virginia's $700 million in cuts for the coming biennium include the state's share of an array of school district operating and capital expenses and funding for class-size reduction in kindergarten through third grade. In addition, a $500 million reduction in state funding for some 13,000 support staff such as janitors, school nurses, and school psychologists from last year's budget was made permanent.
- Washington suspended a program to reduce class sizes and provide professional development for teachers; the state also reduced funding for maintaining 4th grade student-to-staff-ratios by $30 million.
- State education grants to school districts and education programs have also been cut in Alabama, Connecticut, Delaware, the District of Columbia, Florida, Idaho, Indiana, Iowa, Kansas, Kentucky, Maine, Nebraska, Nevada, Ohio, Oregon, Pennsylvania, South Carolina, and Utah.

However, Higher Education is not immune to state cuts, whereby "at least 43 states have implemented cuts to public colleges and universities and/or made large increases in college tuition to make up for insufficient state funding":

Alabama's fiscal year 2011 cuts to higher education have led to 2010–11 tuition hikes that range from 8 percent to 23 percent, depending on the institution

- Arizona's Board of Regents approved in-state undergraduate tuition increases of between 9 and 20 percent as well as fee increases at the state's three public universities. Additionally, the three state universities must implement a 2.75

    percent reduction in state-funded salary spending and plan to do so through a variety of actions, such as academic reorganization, layoffs, furloughs, position eliminations, hiring fewer tenure-eligible faculty, and higher teaching workloads.

- The University of California has increased tuition by 32 percent and reduced freshman enrollment by 2,300 students; the California State University system cut enrollment by 40,000 students.
- Colorado funding for higher education was reduced by $62 million from FY 2010 and this has led to cutbacks at the state's institutions. The University of Colorado system will lay off 79 employees in FY 2011 and has increased employee workloads and required higher employee contributions to health and retirement benefits.
- Florida's 11 public universities will raise tuition by 15 percent for the 2010–11 academic year. This tuition hike, combined with a similar increase in 2009-10, results in a total two-year increase of 32 percent.
- Georgia has cut state funding for public higher education for FY2011 by $151 million, or 7 percent. As a result, undergraduate tuition for the fall 2010 semester at Georgia's four public research universities (Georgia State, Georgia Tech, the Medical College of Georgia, and the University of Georgia) will increase by $500 per semester, or 16 percent. Community college tuition will increase by $50 per semester.
- The University of Idaho has responded to budget cuts by imposing furlough days on 2,600 of its employees statewide. Furloughs will range from 4 hours to 40 hours depending on pay level.
- Indiana's cuts to higher education have caused Indiana State University to plan to lay off 89 staff.
- Michigan has reduced student financial aid by $135 million (over 61 percent), including decreases of 50 percent in competitive scholarships and 44 percent in tuition grants, as well as elimination of nursing scholarships, work-study, the Part-Time Independent Student Program, Michigan Education Opportunity Grants, and the Michigan Promise Scholarships.
- In Minnesota, as a result of higher education funding cuts, approximately 9,400 students will lose their state financial aid grants entirely, and the remaining state financial aid recipients will see their grants cut by 19 percent.
- Missouri's fiscal year 2011 budget reduces by 60 percent funding for the state's only need-based financial aid program, which helps 42,000 students access higher education. This cut was partially restored with other scholarship money, but will still result in a cut of at least 24 percent to need-based aid.
- New Mexico has eliminated over 80 percent of support to the College Affordability Endowment Fund, which provides need-based scholarships to 2,366 students who do not qualify for other state grants or scholarships. New York's state university system has increased resident undergraduate tuition by 14 percent beginning with the spring 2009 semester.
- In North Carolina, University of North Carolina students will see their tuition rise by $750 in the 2010-2011 school year and community college students

will see their tuition increase by $200 due to fiscal year 2011 reductions in state higher education spending.

— South Dakota's fiscal year 2011 budget cuts state support for public universities by $6.5 million and as a result the Board of Regents has increased university tuition by 4.6 percent and cut university programs by $4.4 million.

— Texas has instituted a 5 percent across-the-board budget cut that reduced higher education funding by $73 million.

— Virginia's community colleges implemented a tuition increase during the spring 2010 semester.

— Washington has reduced state funding for the University of Washington by 26 percent for the current biennium. Washington State University is increasing tuition by almost 30 percent over two years. In its supplemental budget, the state cut 6 percent more from direct aid to the state's six public universities and 34 community colleges, which will lead to further tuition increases, administrative cuts, furloughs, layoffs, and other cuts. The state also cut support for college work-study by nearly one-third and suspended funding for a number of its financial aid programs.

— Other states that are cutting higher education operating funding and financial aid include Arkansas, Connecticut, Hawaii, Illinois, Iowa, Kansas, Kentucky, Louisiana, Maine, Maryland, Massachusetts, Mississippi, Nebraska, Nevada, New Jersey, Ohio, Oklahoma, Oregon, Pennsylvania, Rhode Island, South Carolina, Tennessee, Utah, Vermont, and Wisconsin.

He asks, "Have we gone collectively out of our minds? Our young people – their capacities to think, understand, investigate, and innovate – are America's future. In the name of fiscal prudence we're endangering that future" (http://www.csmonitor.com/Business/Robert-Reich/2010/1223/American-education-under-attack).

Education is not only subject to attack in the USA in terms of economic aspects, but has violent dimensions elsewhere as detailed in a UNESCO report of 2010, by Brendan O'Malley, *Education under attack: A global study on targeted political and military violence against education staff, students, teachers, union and government officials, and institutions*, examines "targeted violent attacks, carried out for political, military, ideological, sectarian, ethnic or religious reasons, against students, teachers, academics, education trade unionists, education or religious reasons, against students, teachers, academics, education trade unionists, education officials and all those who work in or for education institutions such as schools, colleges and universities. It also includes attacks on educational buildings, such as the firebombing of schools" (O'Malley, 2010, p. 17). This study indicates the deadliest locations for educators in recent years and that "high rate of assassination of teachers, teacher trade unionists, students and academics remains a matter of grave concern in Colombia, Iraq, Nepal and Thailand. In Colombia, the number of death threats against teachers and the number of threats and killings of university students has risen sharply" (O'Malley, 2010, p. 44). So far the attacks on US educational institutions seem to not be so much politically motivated, but are gun-related attacks by highly disaffected individuals that massacre or injure several people (e.g. Columbine High School, 1999; Virginia Tech, 2007; Northern Illinois University, 2008, and other events that kill fewer people). Nevertheless that laws now propose allowing guns to be carried on some university campuses remains a deeply worrisome concern to me e.g. Texas has proposed a law that allows concealed handguns on site its 38 public colleges with half a million students (*Telegraph*, 2011, http://www.telegraph.co.uk/news/worldnews/northamerica/usa/8338805/Universities-in-Texas-to-allow-students-to-carry-guns-on-campus.html).

CONCLUSION

Education per se, which is far more than K-12 schooling and 'Public Education' is now politicised and more under attack than ever. For youth the privatisation of education is occurring at the very point when education has been profiled as being the basis and central to the Knowledge economy, so the battles of public versus private education have to be fought all over again.

In the light of such major issues facing the economy and in turn education, there are several scenarios:

1. Increased austerity budgeting regardless of who wins the US presidency in 2012. Despite avowed emphases on the importance of education, cuts of various sorts and increases in student fees in higher education are likely.
2. Irrespective of the possible re-election of Obama, children of the poor and the middle class are aware that university education can no longer guarantee either a job or a well paid one, so are increasingly turning away from universities to other possibilities for jobs in trades, media, hospitality. This then poses questions about what will happen with universities, who will attend? What will they study? Who will fund this?
3. Universities are increasingly adopting a form of digital Taylorism as a stripped down model for tuition, using e-learning, buying courses or using professors to create courses, but lower paid, assistants and non-PhD tutors to deliver these.
4. Social media provides opportunities for co-ordinated protest connecting sub-jectivities in ways that make universities more irrelevant.

The USA, like many Western nations has been fairly successful in creating a relatively docile youth population since the Civil Rights and Vietnam war era protests as youth have obediently followed expected paths and promises that a college education was the best way to a good, satisfying, well paying job and to social mobility. As the financial burden has increasingly shifted to youth and their families to fund their higher education, they have increasingly developed an entrepreneurial self where they chose their education to maximize their life chances (see Besley & Peters, 2007). Unfortunately, in the current world wide economic crisis, we have begun to see that in the face of austerity budgets alongside high levels of unemployment for youth and for graduates, that even the middle classes are losing hope. There have already been large demonstrations against austerity measures, increases in student fees, the Occupy Wall Street groups and even riots in many European countries in 2011 (e.g. Greece, Italy, France, Spain and UK). Youth have also seen the power of protest and political action largely co-ordinated through social media in much of the Arab world amid calls for democracy and freedoms as opposed to continued rule by long standing authoritarian dictators and monarchs. So the spectre of youth and others conducting similar actions in the face of increasing loss of hope has to be acknowledged as a strong possibility – all part of the nightmare as the expectation of hope engendered by Obama's election when the financial crisis had already begun, has not improved, but has been transformed to hopelessness only a few years later. Obama may have wonderful rhetoric but as president he faces limited ability to effect change in a democratic system different from parliamentary democracies and other Western democracies, one where federal power is limited by not only the constitution but by political realities. Congress legislates and can refuse to appropriate funds for presidential initiatives and to confirm presidential appointees, such as ambassadors or Supreme Court justices. In the layers of power, it often seems, especially currently, that legislators are far more interested in maintaining their own position than in working together for the common good in caring for others, in favoring a very narrow formulation of self-interest that seems to ignore that care for others is a value implied in care of the self (Besley & Peters, 2007).

NOTES

[1] Youth unemployment rates, 2011 (approx.): Spain, 47%; Eurozone, 21%; USA, 17%; Germany, 9%.

[2] USA defines the poverty line as income of $22,314 a year for a family of four and $11,139 for an individual (US Census Bureau, http://www.census.gov/compendia/statab/cats/income_expenditures_poverty_wealth.html). The poverty rate for children under age 18 increased to 22% in 2010; the poverty rate for adults ages 18 to 64 rose to 13.7%; for people 65 and older, the poverty rate was barely changed at 9%. Non-Hispanic whites had lowest poverty rate, 9.9%; Asians, 12.1%; Hispanic 26.6%; Blacks had the highest rate at 27.4%. About 14% of men were below the poverty line, compared to 16.2% of women. Families headed by a married couple had only a 6.2% poverty rate, whereas families with a single mother had a 31.6% rate, and families with a single father had a 15.8% rate (Annalyn Censky, 2011, http://money.cnn.com/2011/09/13/news/economy/poverty_rate_income/index.htm; http://www.census.gov/compendia/statab/cats/income_expenditures_poverty_wealth.html).

[3] October 15, tens of thousands of demonstrators staged rallies in 900 cities around the world, including Auckland, Sydney, Hong Kong, Taipei, Tokyo, São Paulo, Paris, Madrid, Berlin, Hamburg, Leipzig, and many other cities. Source: http://en.wikipedia.org/wiki/Occupy_Wall_Street.

[4] Early Childhood: 'Zero to Five Plan' fund & help states move toward voluntary, universal preschool education; Expand Early Head Start and Head Start; Provide affordable, High-Quality Child Care. K-12: Reform No Child Left Behind; Support High-Quality Schools and Close Low-Performing Charter Schools; Make Math and Science Education a National Priority; Expand High-Quality Afterschool Opportunities (21st Century Learning Programs); Support College Outreach Programs e.g. GEAR UP, TRIO and Upward Bound; Support College Credit Initiatives; Support English Language Learners; Recruit, Prepare, Retain & Reward Teachers. Higher Education: Create the American Opportunity Tax Credit: universal and fully refundable credit will ensure that the first $4,000 of a college education is completely free for most Americans, and will cover two-thirds the cost of tuition at the average public college or university and make community college tuition completely free for most students. Recipients of the credit will be required to conduct 100 hours of community service; Simplify the Application Process for Financial Aid. (http://change.gov/agenda/education_agenda/)

REFERENCES

Abramson, L. (2011). In *Teaching pink slips are a way of life*, National Public Radio, http://www.npr.org/2011/06/15/137090661/in-teaching-pink-slips-are-a-way-of-life.

Besley, A. C. & Peters, M. A. (2007). *Subjectivity and truth: Foucault, education and the culture of self.* New York: Peter Lang.

Bruce, M. (2011). Wisconsin teachers protested budget, union cuts. *ABC News*, http://abcnews.go.com/Politics/wisconsin-protests-news-wisconsin-governor-scott-walkers-proposal/story?id=12942012#.Tt7mtL8z3Zc.

Censky, A. (2011). Poverty rates rise in America. *CNNMoney*, http://money.cnn.com/2011/09/13/news/economy/poverty_rate_income/index.htm.

Line, M. (2011). Providence plans to pink slip all teachers. *Liveshots*, http://liveshots.blogs.foxnews.com/2011/02/24/providence-plans-to-pink-slip-all-teachers/#ixzz1evnTU63G.

O'Malley, B. (2010). *Education under attack: A global study on targeted political and military violence against education staff, students, teachers, union and government officials, and institutions.* Paris: UNESCO. www.unesdoc.unesco.org/images/0018/001868/186809e.pdf.

Reich, R. (2010). American education under attack. *Christian Science Monitor*, http://www.csmonitor.com/Business/Robert-Reich/2010/1223/American-education-under-attack.

Todd, C. (2009). Understanding Obama's education vision. *FirstRead on MSNBC*, http://firstread.msnbc.msn.com/_news/2009/03/12/4424745-understanding-obamas-education-vision.

Websites:

ABC News (2011). http://abclocal.go.com/kabc/story?section=news/state&id=6710423.

Alice Cooper, Welcome to my nightmare lyrics. http://www.elyrics.net/read/a/alice-cooper-lyrics/welcome-to-my-nightmare-lyrics.html.

CBS News (2011). http://www.cbsnews.com/stories/2011/03/16/national/main20043778.shtml.

Congressional Budget Office (October, 2011). Trends in the distribution of household income between 1979 and 2007. http://www.cbo.gov/doc.cfm?index=12485.

Office of the President-Elect. Agenda – Education, The Obama–Biden Plan, Change.Gov. http://change.gov/agenda/education_agenda/.

Occupy Wall Street, Wikipedia. http://en.wikipedia.org/wiki/Occupy_Wall_Street.

Reason TV (2011). 3 reasons Obama's education vision deserves an F. Big Government. http://biggovernment.com/reasontv/2010/10/09/3-reasons-obamas-education-vision-deserves-an-f/.

Telegraph (2011). Universities in Texas 'to allow students to carry guns on campus'. http://www.telegraph.co.uk/news/worldnews/northamerica/usa/8338805/Universities-in-Texas-to-allow-students-to-carry-guns-on-campus.html

US Census Bureau (2011). The 2012 Statistical Abstract: Income, expenditures, poverty, & wealth. http://www.census.gov/compendia/statab/cats/income_expenditures_poverty_wealth.html.

Printed in the United States
By Bookmasters